RIVERS IN AMERICAN LIFE AND TIMES

THE MISSOURI RIVER

Tim McNeese

CHELSEA HOUSE
PUBLISHERS

A Haights Cross Communications Company

Philadelphia

FRONTIS: Map of the Upper Mississippi and Missouri Rivers by M. Souland, 1795

CHELSEA HOUSE PUBLISHERS

VP, NEW PRODUCT DEVELOPMENT   Sally Cheney
DIRECTOR OF PRODUCTION   Kim Shinners
CREATIVE MANAGER Takeshi Takahashi
MANUFACTURING MANAGER Diann Grasse

Staff for THE MISSOURI RIVER

EXECUTIVE EDITOR Lee Marcott
PRODUCTION EDITOR Megan Emery
PHOTO EDITOR Sarah Bloom
SERIES DESIGNER Keith Trego
COVER DESIGNER Keith Trego
LAYOUT 21st Century Publishing and Communications, Inc.

A Haights Cross Communications Company

www.chelseahouse.com

First Printing

9 8 7 6 5 4 3 2 1

Library of Congress Cataloging-in-Publication Data applied for.

ISBN 0-7910-7724-1 HC   0-7910-8007-2 PB

CONTENTS

1

The River and
Its Early People

Its waters trickle down from the ancient peaks of the Rocky Mountains across endless tracts of the Great Plains, forming a river longer than any other in the United States. The Missouri River of today measures approximately 2,500 miles in length from its Montana headwaters to its union with the Mississippi River north of St. Louis, Missouri. It is longer than the great Mississippi by a couple of hundred miles, even though the Missouri is today a couple of hundred miles shorter than its course of a century ago. (The Mississippi River is a larger river, however, containing more water than any other in North America.) Above the site where the two rivers join together, north of St. Louis, the Missouri River is twice as long as the Upper Mississippi. The Missouri River watershed drains an area covering approximately 530,000 square miles, a landmass equal to one-sixth of the entire United States. The banks of the Missouri river touch seven states, including Montana, North Dakota, South Dakota, Nebraska, Iowa, Kansas, and Missouri.

The amount of water that flows down the Missouri River annually amounts to as much as 8.4 trillion gallons. The volume of the river is enough to cover 25 million acres of land with a foot of water. As one biologist has noted, "The average water use in the United States is one hundred gallons a day per person. With each person using one hundred gallons a day, the Missouri's flow is enough to provide water for domestic and public use for about 230 million people,"[1] just 40 million people short of the entire population of the United States.

Nearly a century ago, while the river was still in its primitive, natural state, the writer George Fitch described the Missouri as "the hungriest river ever created."[2] For hundreds, perhaps thousands, of years, the Missouri was an untamed waterway, its silt-laden water twisting and turning back on itself like a giant snake. Its currents chewed up riverbanks, causing constant collapse and rerouting. Trees along its banks regularly fell in as the banks themselves disappeared into the river, adding to its mud content and helping provide one of the river's many nicknames: Big Muddy.

Two hundred years ago, as the explorers Meriwether Lewis and William Clark led their men up the river in search of the unknown lands of the American West, the Missouri was noted for its wild, unruly nature. It was a river thick with sandbars, choked with submerged trees and shifting currents. The Missouri River as it flows today is largely a tamed river. Although a few hundred miles of its course still follow the Missouri's natural floodplain, creating and recreating its primary channel as well as its feeders and peripheral streams, the river has been coaxed to calmness, its violent, voracious tendencies now quieted by a series of six major dams. In addition, the lower reaches of the river, throughout the twentieth century, have been channelized and narrowed, the bottom standardized to a common depth of nine feet, all for the purpose of making the river navigable to commercial barge traffic. Such traffic never fully developed, but the river remains at ease, artificially manipulated to serve its human residents. As such, the Missouri is tapped in a variety of ways:

> The modern Missouri River serves millions of people. It provides irrigation water to farmers in Montana, hydroelectricity to city folk in Great Falls, Sioux City, and Omaha, walleye for sport fishers in the Dakotas, drinking water for the thirsty cattle of ranchers in Nebraska, and an occasional navigable water route for barge companies based in St. Louis. Only within the past 100 years has the river been engineered and managed to provide these benefits; the intensive use of the Missouri River is a twentieth-century phenomenon. The waterscape of the modern Missouri reflects the diverse individuals and interest groups it serves each day.[3]

The Missouri is such an extensive river in length that in order to be comprehended, it must be divided, The Upper Missouri begins as three rivers, the Jefferson, Gallatin, and Madison Rivers—all named by the early nineteenth-century American explorers Lewis and Clark—come together to form the river's headwaters in western Montana. As it twists and

NAMING THE MISSOURI RIVER

Any modern-day map or globe will identify the great river flowing across America's heartland as the Missouri River. Throughout history, however, the name for this lengthy North American waterway has varied from one people to another and from one era to the next.

The river was first named by its earliest inhabitants, the various tribes of Native Americans that lived on its banks or used the river as a highway across the Great Plains. The Hidatsa tribe called the river "Anati," which has been translated as "navigable stream full of dirt." The Lakota agreed with the Hidatsa when they named the river "Mini Sose," which means "Muddy Water." The Omaha called it "Smoky River." Another group of Indians, the Mandan, referred to the river as "Mata," translated as "boundary between two pieces of land."

Europeans who reached the waters of the Missouri gave the river different names, including the "River of the Osages," after a Native American tribal group. In 1712, the king of France called the waterway, "The River St. Philip, heretofore called Missouri."

Early French explorers referred to the great waterway as "the river of the Missouris," naming it after yet another important tribe of Native Americans living along the Lower Missouri. How the word "Missouri" should be translated is a mystery. Some experts believe that the word means "Big Muddy," a common modern-day reference to the river. Others believe that the word was derived from an Illinois Indian word meaning "wooden canoe."

As names have come and gone, however, the name "Missouri," perhaps one of the oldest, remains the river's designated name, one that will likely remain for all time.

turns along its course across Montana, the northern Great Plains of the Dakotas, and eastern Nebraska, the river is fed by several western waterways including the Yellowstone, Niobrara, and Platte Rivers, until it reaches its largest city: Omaha, Nebraska.

The river then becomes the Lower Missouri as it flows over the central Great Plains of interior North America, where cottonwood bottomlands huddle along the river as it reaches the prairie country of central Missouri, a still rural portion of the river, where small towns punctuate the Missouri's course,

Though the Missouri River is now largely tamed, when explorers first arrived it was swift and unruly, filled with sandbars, silt and mud, shifting currents and submerged trees. This painting shows the river in the nineteenth century.

sharing the Lower Missouri with larger, metropolitan communities such as Kansas City.

Over the past several centuries, the Missouri River developed into one of the great rivers of the American West. Towns sprang up along its banks, some destined to become major western cities, including Kansas City, Missouri, and Omaha, Nebraska. Other smaller, less-significant towns also developed along the river, becoming important regional centers of commerce and settlement, such as Sioux City, Iowa; Bismarck, North Dakota; St. Joseph, Missouri; Jefferson City, Missouri's state capital; and St. Charles, Missouri, situated near the river's mouth. The river also provided the sites for four state capitals, including Jefferson City, Missouri; Pierre, South Dakota; Bismarck, North Dakota; and Helena, Montana. Today, the Missouri River basin is home to 11 million people who rely on the river for commerce, industry, recreation, and, of course, drinking water. The river remains one of the most vital natural resources for those living in proximity of its banks.

Geologically, the ancient Missouri River altered course even more dramatically than its modern-day counterpart. According to geologists, the Upper Missouri originally flowed across the Northern Great Plains to the northeast, toward Canada and Hudson Bay, rather than to the southeast, as it does today. Through long stretches of geological time, the ancient Missouri's current cut deep channels through canyons running up to 1,000 feet deep. Through a process known as downcutting, the ancient river exposed both sedimentary and igneous rock layers, creating new courses. Much of the rock located along the Upper Missouri River is sedimentary, created from marine muds and sands. As these sedimentary rocks were deposited across central, modern-day Montana, they were covered with waters that made up the Western Interior Seaway. For hundreds of thousands of years, currents and natural oscillations caused this prehistoric water system to change in shape and content. Over time, the seaway deposited great rock layers of shale, sandstone, and siltstone that ultimately provided the major valley walls and cliffs that today define the course of the Upper Missouri.

It was a lengthy period of glaciation—a geological event commonly called an "Ice Age"—that established much of the modern Missouri River. As recently as 10,000 years ago, great glaciers of ice ground slowly across the North American continent, causing the ancient Missouri to alter its course and begin moving south, away from Canada. Near the confluence of the Yellowstone and Missouri Rivers (near the border of eastern Montana and western North Dakota), the glaciers turned the river, creating a great horseshoe bend and redirecting its modern course toward the central Mississippi River.

This prehistoric "right turn" for the Missouri River recreated its course, but it would provide an uneasy bed for a turbulent river. The Missouri became "a hopeful, pushing, enterprising stream; but after it joined forces with the turbid Yellowstone, it seems to have lost its clear purpose, though increasing its original force."[4] The glacial-scarred landscape of the modern-day Dakotas, Nebraska, Iowa, and northern Missouri provided an open valley region that left the Missouri to finger its way across a relatively flattened region, giving the river an opportunity to fan out, creating multiple new channels, a tangle of watery arteries that paralleled one another, challenged each for supremacy, and ultimately created a river with almost no boundaries.

The earliest inhabitants of the region watered by the Missouri River and its many tributaries were the original peoples of the Western Hemisphere, the Native Americans, or Indians. Anthropologists date many of the first Indian arrivals to the Missouri River region, and to the Great Plains in general, as early as 10,000 B.C. These were hunter–gatherer cultures, mostly nomadic hunter groups—small bands of people, usually several combined family groups—who stalked the great Pleistocene animals, including woolly mammoths, toward the end of the most recent Ice Age. The Great Plains played host to thousands of these small bands of migratory hunters.

Beginning around 7000 B.C., and for the next 2,500 years, the Great Plains experienced a heat wave, sending many of the native animals out of the region to more hospitable environments in the Rockies and east of the Mississippi River. Many of the human inhabitants of the Great Plains also abandoned the drought-stricken region. Those who remained subsisted as small-game hunters and trappers. This period saw little human activity, and it was not until the third millennium B.C. that the numbers of Native Americans living on the Great Plains increased by any significant numbers. By 2500 B.C., eastern influences, the Mound Builders of the Mississippi Valley, were returning to the Great Plains, using the Missouri River to make their way into the Plains interior. Repopulating the Great Plains took many generations of occupation.

Between 500 B.C. and A.D. 1000—known by anthropologists as the Plains Woodland Period—a fairly advanced village existence had developed on the Plains, and significant sites included those located along the Missouri River's banks near modern-day Kansas City, Missouri. The Native Americans of this era planted significant crop fields, growing corn and beans and creating one of the first eras of systematic Indian agriculture in North America. Groups of Plains Indians lived along the Missouri River Valley, including in eastern Kansas and Nebraska. By A.D. 800, the Woodland cultures had become more reliant on agriculture as a food source, had become more sedentary, and relied on the Missouri River for transportation, communication, and trade.

After A.D. 800, important Native American groups settled along the Missouri River. Siouan-speakers arrived in the Missouri Valley from east of the Mississippi. Others arrived from the Southern Plains. Over several centuries, the Plains Indians of the Missouri River region developed greater reliance on their improved farming techniques, growing fields of corn, beans, squash, and sunflowers in the bottomlands along the river. They lived in permanent housing, typically "earth-covered or mud-plastered lodges, usually square or rectangular in shape, cultivated their gardens with digging sticks and bison-scapula hoes, stored their surplus food in underground pits, and often surrounded their villages with protective stockades and ditches."[5]

By A.D. 1500, Native Americans lived in scattered settlements along several parts of the Missouri River. Their lodges had changed by then, as they were adapted into circular mounds covered with prairie grass. These new houses

> were distinctive Plains circular dwellings with 4, 6, 8, or even 10 central roof support posts around a central hearth. The walls consisted of peripheral posts against which other posts leaned inward. The walls were covered with grass and finally with a thick layer of earth that continued onto the roof, leaving only a central opening for the escape of smoke from the central hearth. A tunnel-like entry passage projected from an east or south wall.[6]

This became the pattern along the middle region of the Missouri and across the Central Plains. With the arrival of non-Indians into the region by the seventeenth century, Plains Indians had developed complex political systems, as well as extensive trade connections, using the Missouri River as their major highway.

The common Indian means of transportation on the Missouri River was not the stereotypical Native American birch bark canoe. Such trees were not abundant enough in the region generally, and the relatively flimsy frame of these early American rivercraft did not perform well on the turbulent Missouri River. Instead, the Missouri River natives carved dugout canoes—boats hacked from a single tree trunk. Dugouts were constructed by "gouging out or burning out the inside of a log into a thin wooden shell."[7] An average design might feature a canoe with a beam of two or three feet and large enough to accommodate three boatmen. Such a three-man crew of Native Americans generally included one paddling from the bow of the boat, one sitting amidships, and a third sitting at the stern, where he could steer the boat. The size of such dugouts might vary considerably, and those made on the Lower Missouri were often quite large. The American artist George Caleb Bingham, while touring the Missouri

River region in 1845, painted one canvas depicting a dugout canoe 12 feet in length. Such canoes had their drawbacks—they were heavy to lug around and they could be awkward to maneuver in the water—but they were built to last and were practically indestructible. They worked well on the Missouri because they could pass over sandbars and snags without significant damage.

Another popular Plains Indians river craft was a boat covered with animal hides, called a bullboat. Small and simple in design, the bullboat or skinboat consisted of a wooden framework covered over with buffalo hides, which were sewn tightly together with animal sinew. The hide seams were covered over with gumbo mud or buffalo fat to keep the sinew dry and render the boat somewhat watertight, at least for a short time. The boats were easy to build and commonly used, but they did not last long. The hides did not keep water out well, and the frames rotted quickly. They could be used for a trip or two across the Missouri or other western rivers and then could be easily discarded and replaced.

When white Europeans arrived in the region of the Missouri River, they discovered a river used by dozens of Native American tribes. Along the Lower Missouri, in modern-day Missouri and Kansas, lived several Siouan-speaking tribes, including the Osage, Missouri, Kansa, Otoe, Omaha, Ioway, and Ponca. By the early 1700s, the Omaha, Ponca, Otoe, and Missouri lived in villages of as many as 2,000 people along the western banks of the Missouri in modern-day Nebraska.

Along the Upper Missouri were the Caddoan-speaking Arikara and Siouan-speaking Mandan and Hidatsa. Along various tributaries of the Missouri, the Pawnee had migrated north into Nebraska. Farther north, various bands of Lakota peoples had gathered in close proximity to the Missouri River, including the Yankton Lakota who lived along the river in southern South Dakota. Along the Upper Missouri, other Native American culture groups could be found. Between the Missouri and the Yellowstone Rivers lived the Siouan Crow tribe, who

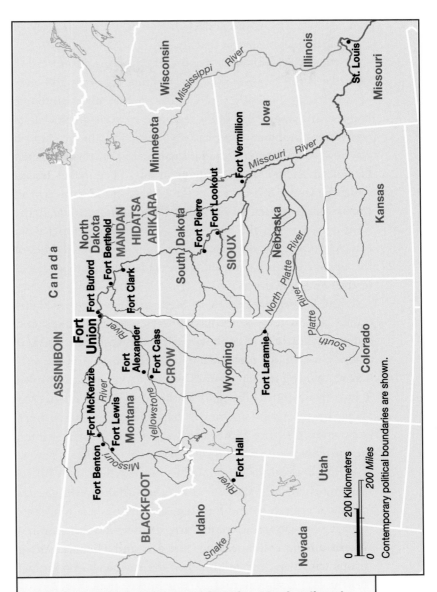

The Missouri River and its many tributaries extend northwest from St. Louis, Missouri, across the Great Plains. This contemporary map shows the path of the river and names, in yellow, some of the dozens of Native American tribes that made their homes along the river's banks.

had separated from the Hidatsa earlier in the 1700s after an intertribal squabble over a buffalo.

In the Upper Missouri region of Montana, other tribes dominated the hunting grounds, farming territory, and river commerce. By the early 1700s, tribes such as the Assiniboine and the Cree had settled in the region of western North Dakota and eastern Montana. They had previously lived in the Hudson Bay region of French Canada but had migrated west in the face of advancing European populations. These tribes traded along the Upper Missouri with the Blackfoot and Gros Ventres further upriver, often serving as middlemen in the trade. In the same way, later in the eighteenth century, the Teton Lakota (Sioux) became the dominant force along the lower reaches of the Upper Missouri, controlling the trade between those tribes upriver and downriver.

By the 1700s, many of these Missouri River–Great Plains tribes had developed extensive agricultural systems and sedentary lifestyles. Then a new element was added to their culture, which, for some, changed their world dramatically before making direct contact with Europeans: the horse. A European import brought to the New World during the 1500s by the Spanish, horses had reached the Southern Great Plains by the 1680s and, just two generations later, the animals could be found even on the Northern Plains. The horse brought these tribes unparalleled mobility, allowing them to systematically hunt buffalo. With greater reliance on horse-bound hunting, some tribes again became at least semi-nomadic, remaining in their earthen-mound villages during colder months and leaving their villages for annual hunting forays on horseback that might last months. With the arrival of the horse, tribes along the Missouri tended to rely less on the river for their mobility. Their use of the horse also encouraged many tribes to engage in repeated wars with one another, raiding their enemies' camps, stealing their horses, and generally destroying their villages.

As Europeans and later Americans reached the Missouri River by the 1700s and early 1800s, they found a unique world of Native Americans, whom they called "Indians," who had developed well-defined social practices, farming techniques, trade systems, and patterns of village life. Much of that Native American world would not survive the arrival of the non-Indian visitors.

2

New Faces
on the River

For hundreds of years, dozens of Native American tribal groups, from farming communities to hunting societies, occupied the various valleys of the Missouri River. All of these Indian tribes used the river and its tributaries for transportation and trade. Long-standing trade alliances remained in place from one generation to the next. Several tribes dominated the trade in their regions, such as the Blackfoot along the Upper Missouri, the Teton Lakota (Sioux) along the Middle Missouri, and the Osage in the Lower Missouri Valley. With the advance of non-Indians into the Missouri River region by the 1600s, the world of Indian trade along the Missouri was bound to change.

The first white Europeans of record to reach the banks of the Missouri included a party of Frenchmen, including the famed Jesuit priest Father Jacques Marquette. His arrival and "discovery" of the Missouri River were nearly accidental and are otherwise incidental. He and his group of French boatmen, including Louis Joliet, were exploring the Upper Mississippi River in the spring of 1673. As they approached the great confluence of the two American rivers, Father Marquette was both fearful of and awestruck by the sight of the Big Muddy. He recorded his surprise in his journal:

> As we were gently sailing down the still clear water [of the Mississippi], we heard a noise of a rapid into which we were about to fall. I have seen nothing more frightful, a mass of large trees entire with branches, real floating islands came from Pekitanoui, so impetuous that we could not without great danger expose ourselves to pass across. The agitation was so great that the water was all muddy, and could not get clear.[8]

Despite having reached one of the most important of the western rivers in America, Father Marquette and Joliet did not explore the river further. It would be left to other, later French explorers to provide the impetus for more French interest in the Missouri River.

The first Europeans to record reaching Missouri were French explorers Jacques Marquette and Louis Joliet. Marquette and Joliet actually found the river by accident during their 1673 exploration of the Mississippi River, seen in this engraving. They were awestruck by the dangerous, muddy river and chose not to explore it further.

Although the voyage of discovery of Marquette and Joliet is well-documented, no one knows definitively who the first European was to reach the banks of the Missouri River. By the 1600s, French fur traders, known as *coureurs du bois* (which literally translates as "runners of the woods") were active in the region of the Missouri, trading with Indians. There are vague accounts of other French explorers who floated up the Missouri as early as the 1680s. According to one of the great French explorers and colonizers of North America, René-Robert Cavelier de La Salle, a pair of French coureurs du bois had reached the Missouri River as early as 1680 or 1681. According to a rumor of the day, the two independently operating traders had been captured by Missouri Indians and delivered to their village. La Salle also wrote of a second pair of French coureurs du bois who, in 1683, had reached the Missouri and lived with the Kaskaskia, Missouri, and Osage tribes, somewhere along the Lower Missouri in modern-day Missouri state.

A decade later, more stories circulated of another pair of French traders who were led up the Missouri in the spring of 1693. Several Kaskaskia Indians from east of the Mississippi accompanied the Frenchmen to the lands of the Missouri tribe. The French intended to establish friendly relations with the Missouri and strike a trade agreement. Five years later, another Jesuit priest, Father St. Cosme, reached the Missouri and traveled upriver, making missionary contacts with several Lower Missouri tribes.

More than 40 years passed before the next important European discoverer reached the Missouri. In the spring of 1714, another Frenchman, Etienne Venyard de Bourgmont, began a voyage up the Missouri and became the first European "to explore, chart, and describe the Missouri above the villages of the Missouri Indians."[9] He reached the Missouri while the Missouri Indians were encamped near the Utz site, situated along river bluffs near the mouth of the Grand River, which flowed into the Missouri from the north. Bourgmont remained with the Missouri and Osage Indians for the next five years, eventually taking the daughter of a Missouri chief as his wife. Bourgmont kept a journal, recording things he saw and experienced that gave him insight into the lifestyle and mind of the Indians with whom he lived. The young Frenchman described the Osage as "a splendid race, and more alert than any other nation."[10] During these years of river prairie experience, Bourgmont was constantly awed at the attractiveness of the land and the bounty of the game and the customs of his Indian hosts. In one entry, he noted, "The meadows are rolling like the sea and abound with wild animals . . . in such quantities as to surpass the imagination.

All the tribes hunt with the arrow; they have splendid horses and are good riders."[11]

By 1719, he had returned to France and was appointed as the Commandant de la Rivière du Missouri. The following year, he returned to the Lower Missouri with instructions to establish relations with any Indians upriver he could, including the Kansa and a band of Apache, then rumored to be living in modern-day Kansas. Delays kept Bourgmont from reconnecting with his old friends, the Missouri, until 1723. By then, he and his fellow French comrades had established a fortified post called Fort Orleans, near the Grand River–Missouri River junction, close to the Missouri Indian encampment.

During the summer of 1724, Bourgmont was able to outfit an expedition of men and supplies to explore farther upriver. He had been dispatched up the river as part of a French effort to sway several key river tribes away from increasing Spanish influence coming up from Santa Fe to the southwest. Bourgmont arrived at the Kansa villages along the Kansas River, south of present-day Kansas City, Kansas. His meeting with the Kansa went well, although the diplomacy took a few awkward turns. The Kansa were intent on establishing trade connections with the French, and Bourgmont discussed trade possibilities with seven different Kansa chiefs. They showered Bourgmont with gifts, including a pair of smoking pipes. One of the chiefs offered him a different kind of present: his 14-year-old daughter. When the Frenchman refused, explaining that he was already married, the chief offered the adolescent girl to Bourgmont's ten-year-old Missouri Indian son, stating, "[your son] will be our head chief, and you will be our true father [protector]."[12]

Through additional negotiations, the French party and the Kansa chiefs concluded important agreements. Bourgmont proceeded farther up river. He reached the site of modern-day Atchison, Kansas, and then set out overland to the west, where he reached the Apache in north-central Kansas, with whom he was able to make a peace and trade treaty, including setting a price for horses "at a rate of three to one for buffalo robes."[13]

The mission to the Apache completed, Bourgmont left the Missouri River region and returned to France once again, taking with him a diplomatic party of Missouri, Osage, Otoe, and Illinois chiefs. His Missouri Indian wife accompanied him as well. Bourgmont presented them to the court of the French monarch, Louis XV. The presentation of these Native Americans sparked much curiosity among those in the royal court. Dressed in European clothing, including laced waistcoats and tricorner cocked hats, the Indians were wined and dined with great hospitality. Several were taken on a hunting party and "killed a deer in the Bois de Boulogne."[14] They even provided their European hosts with some of their own dances, which they performed at the Paris Opera House and the Théâtre Italien. One of the chiefs, an Illinois leader named Chicagou, later noted how he had found the scent of French perfume repulsive. He described the men and women of King Louis's court as having "smelled like alligators."[15]

Ultimately, Bourgmont's efforts with the Indians of the Lower Missouri helped pave the way for an increased number of French coureurs du bois to continue and extend their fur trading efforts with the Indians in the region of modern-day Missouri.

One of the first recorded European contacts with the Indians on the Upper Missouri was again a Frenchman. In 1783, Pierre Gaultier de Varennes, Sieur de La Verendrye, arrived on the banks of the Upper Missouri after reaching the region from Canada. Although others had probably reached the Upper Missouri before Verendrye, especially the coureurs du bois, he is the first to record his findings. He reached the encampments of the "Mantannes," the tribe known as the Mandan, in the Missouri River region of present-day North Dakota. He found the Indians there hospitable and wrote of his astonishment at the large numbers of wild game and the presence of the great shaggy beasts of the Plains—the bison.

The names of some eighteenth-century European explorers of the Missouri River, such as Bourgmont and Verendrye, are recorded, but others will forever remain nameless. They were the common French trappers and traders—the coureurs du bois—

Though their voyages were not documented, French fur traders were active in the Missouri River region by the late 1600s. By the early seventeenth century, the French had formed settlements and established relations with Native Americans. This painting by George Caleb Bingham depicts fur traders descending the Missouri.

and it seems at times that they were everywhere along the Missouri River during the 1700s.

The future of France's dominance of the Missouri trade over its European rivals, such as Great Britain and Spain, took a serious turn by the 1760s. In 1762, the French government secretly turned over possession of their vast land claims west of the Mississippi River, the great territory of Louisiana, which stretched from the Gulf of Mexico to British-held Canada to the northern Rocky Mountains, to the Spanish. The Mississippi River formed Louisiana's eastern boundary, and the remainder of the region included all the western lands watered by the rivers flowing east from the Rockies and into the Mississippi or its tributaries, the largest of which was the Missouri. The French were fearful that they might lose the war they had been fighting with the British since the mid-1750s and were hoping to quietly hand off Louisiana to the Spanish to keep it out of British hands in case they lost the war completely. France did lose the next war, the French and Indian War, and the resulting negotiations produced the Treaty of Paris, which forced the French to surrender all their territory east of the Mississippi, including Canada. (This war was not fought only in America, but also in much of Europe, where it was called the Seven Years' War.)

Spanish control of Louisiana would not last after the latter decades of the eighteenth century. In October 1800, the French government, led by the dominant Corsican general Napoleon Bonaparte, regained control of Louisiana by forcing Spain to accept a new agreement, the Treaty of San Ildefonso. With that treaty, Louisiana was closed to American immigration. Despite the treaty, the Spanish did not surrender immediate control of the region, but they altered their policies toward the Americans in other ways, at the insistence of the French. By 1802, the Spanish Intendant in New Orleans closed off the port of New Orleans to all American river traffic down the Mississippi. The port could no longer be used "as a place of deposit for merchandise," or "free transit for ships down the river to the sea." [16]

The closing of the Mississippi raised concerns among Americans living in the trans-Appalachian frontier, but by 1803, a new treaty eliminated the challenge. That year, American diplomats Robert Livingston and James Monroe, a future U.S. president, negotiated with the French for the purchase of the Louisiana Territory. By then, Napoleon's dream of a new French empire in North America had died, along with the majority of the troops he had sent to the Americas to establish a military presence at New Orleans. Those seasoned veterans of Napoleon's European battles were virtually wiped out by malaria and yellow fever while stationed on the Caribbean island of Santo Domingo. By the end of the year, French officials in New Orleans had handed over the vast Louisiana Territory to the Americans.

With the transfer of Louisiana to the United States, President Thomas Jefferson was intent on sending Americans into the region for the purposes of exploration. On January 18, 1803, President Jefferson requested from Congress authorization and an appropriation of $2,500 to send a military and scientific expedition to explore up the Missouri River to its source and then down the nearest westward-flowing stream to the Pacific. There was even a possibility in Jefferson's mind that the Missouri might flow clear to the Pacific, representing the long-sought "Northwest Passage." Ironically, when Jefferson sent his message to Congress, none of the territory he wanted explored lay within the United States, but at the very moment he was maturing his plans for a transcontinental exploring expedition, his representatives were negotiating the purchase of Louisiana from Napoleon. With unexpected twists of fate, the two ventures conveniently coincided.

To command the expedition, Jefferson selected his private secretary, Meriwether Lewis, lately of the First U.S. Infantry Regiment. Lewis, with the concurrence of the president, invited his old friend, William Clark, to serve as co-captain. Lewis and Clark had served in the army together during the 1790s. Clark quickly accepted: "This is an undertaking fraited with many difeculties, but My friend I do assure you that no man lives with whome I would perfur to undertake Such a Trip &c. as yourself." [17] (Although Clark was an excellent frontiersman and soldier and proved to be a skilled mapmaker during the expedition, he was an atrocious speller!)

Although the War Department never approved Clark's captaincy, Lewis treated his comrade as an equal in the field. The two men truly led side by side. Their partnership and leadership of the Corps of Discovery along the entire length of the Missouri River from its mouth to its headwaters would alter the history of the great western waterway forever.

A RIVER WITH NO BOUNDARIES

Throughout the history of the Missouri River, the waterway has changed course many times, rearranging itself in new channels and streambeds so that each generation experienced a new river. Geologists and hydrologists refer to these natural alterations in the course of a river as "meanderings." All rivers running along lowlands are prone to meander, and the Missouri is one river famous for it. Although the river's channelization in the twentieth century has cut out the majority of its tendencies to meander, parts of the Missouri remain free to recreate themselves.

One of the most common results of a meander is the formation of an oxbow lake. A meander causes a bend in the river. As the river turns on itself, erosion on the inside banks and soil deposits on the outside banks cause the bases of the bend to gradually close off the neck of the meander. As the neck of the meander is choked off, the river breaks through, sometimes forming two channels—one flowing through the meander loop and the other along the newly connected channel. In time, the new channel lays down enough sediment deposits to cut off the meander, leaving a single channel. The portion of the river that becomes isolated from the river's main course becomes an oxbow lake.

The men on the Lewis and Clark Expedition experienced the Missouri and its many meanders, which caused them to follow a river that snaked and coiled nearly back on itself at several places. During the summer of 1804, along the Great Bend of the Missouri in central South Dakota, the Corps of Discovery completed approximately 25 miles of the river, struggling against the current onboard their keelboat, only to discover that the river had twisted so much that "a man could get to the same point by walking just 700 meters"[*] from one bend in the river to the next.

Channelization has eliminated most of the wild parts of the Missouri, but a few remain. The stretch located between the headwaters of the river and Fort Peck Reservoir (which includes the Missouri National Wild and Scenic River) is as unspoiled and natural in its courses as it was centuries ago. Other untamed, meandering sections of the river include the 40 miles between Fort Randall Dam and Lewis and Clark Lake (at Niobrara, Nebraska), as well as the 60 miles between Ponca, Nebraska, and Gavin's Point Dam.

* Quoted in "America Looks West: Lewis and Clark on the Missouri," *Nebraskaland Magazine* 80, no. 7 (August–September 2002): 47.

3

The Corps
of Discovery

The year 1803 brought extraordinary change to the Missouri River as Americans prepared to ascend its entire length, led by men appointed by the president of the United States himself. Lewis and Clark hired men to accompany them on their important expedition up the Missouri River, and they knew their crew would need to include skilled hunters, rivermen, blacksmiths, carpenters, soldiers, and interpreters. In the end, they pulled together a group of 30 men including 17 regular soldiers, 11 additional enlistees, a half-Indian interpreter named George Drouillard to help the men communicate with upriver Indian tribes, and Clark's manservant, York, a black slave Clark had known since boyhood. Also, the captains hired six additional soldiers—a corporal and five privates—plus several French boatmen to accompany the main party for the first year of the expedition and then return down the Missouri River with any correspondence and collected specimens Lewis wanted delivered to President Jefferson.

Before embarking on this historic journey, Captain Lewis spent months collecting the necessary equipment the men would need for the expedition. By July 1803, Lewis had left Pittsburgh, traveling down the Ohio River on a large keelboat. The keelboat measured 55 feet long and 8 feet wide, carried 12 tons of cargo, and drew between three and four feet of water. He picked up Clark and several recruits at Louisville, Kentucky, and the party proceeded down the Ohio to the Mississippi River. They landed across the Mississippi from the small river town of St. Louis and established their winter camp at Wood River, Illinois, across from the mouth of the Missouri River. During the five winter months, Lewis and Clark recruited other men and trained them. They collected additional supplies and equipment. They met with traders and French boatmen who had been up the Missouri River to find out what to expect when they began their epic journey. By April 1, 1804, the two captains and their party of nearly 50 men were prepared to embark on the greatest adventure of their lives—exploring the Missouri River and the lands to the west. Three craft had been prepared—the keelboat

Despite harsh environmental conditions, illness, and some problems with Indians, Lewis and Clark successfully completed their journey, exploring the lands between the Missouri River and the Pacific Ocean from 1804–1806. This map drawn by William Clark shows the extent of their track across the American frontier.

and two pirogues (large canoes). As they set out on that first morning, it was raining.

Traveling up the Missouri proved to be difficult. The boats sailed when possible for most of the river, but the men had to row against the current. When the boats reached any rapids, the men went ashore and pulled the boats upstream with ropes. By mid-June, however, the crew had settled into a routine that included anticipating rapids along the Missouri. They met with Indians along the river, including the Osage, who were friendly and traded deer meat to the expedition for whiskey. Still, problems were never far from the experiences of the Lewis and Clark party. Storms on the river were a recurring hazard, as were submerged tree trunks and branches in the river, which threatened to tear the bottoms out of their boats. The heat was fierce, and the men fell victim to heat stroke. Captain Clark complained in his journal how "The Ticks & Musquiters [mosquitoes] are verry troublesome."[18] One of the men was bitten by a rattlesnake. Because most of the men regularly spent much of their time in the river pulling the keelboat upstream, their clothes rarely dried out from one day to the next, causing many to develop sores and lesions and even boils on their bodies. Discipline among the young men on the expedition sometimes required the captains to mete out military punish-ments. In late June, one soldier was given 50 lashes for stealing whiskey from the expedition's stock. Another received 100 lashes when he was discovered drunk while on sentry duty; another received the same number for sleeping at his post.

During the final days of June, the Corps passed the site where Kansas City, Missouri stands today, at the confluence of the Kansas and Missouri rivers. As the men explored the lands near the river, they found great open prairies and extensive grasslands that seemed to stretch for miles into the distance. The rolling scenery was dotted with large herds of elk, antelope, and, most important, bison. One herd was huge, with Captain Lewis estimating the number near 10,000. Sergeant John Ordway described the alluring landscape as "one of the most beautiful places I ever Saw in my life, open and beautifully Diversified with hills & vallies all presenting themselves to the River." [19] On the Fourth of July, near modern-day Atchison, Kansas, the men celebrated, firing their guns and dancing to fiddle music played by one of the French boatmen.

By mid-July a great storm nearly destroyed the party's keelboat, the largest vessel the Corps used on the expedition. In a squall of high winds, with thunder and lightning rolling across the darkened skies, the men fought to keep the boat from capsizing and being destroyed. A week later, the party reached the mouth of the Platte River, where they began to see signs of Indians, including abandoned lodges and burial mounds.

From July 22 to 27, 1804, the expedition stopped along the Missouri to rest, dry out the cargo and their clothes, fashion new canoe paddles, catch up on their journals, and find the Indians they knew were close by. Lewis and Clark sent two of their men—George Drouillard, who was half Shawnee, and Private Pierre Cruzatte, whose mother was an Omaha Indian—to go out and find the Otoe. A few days later, Drouillard and Cruzatte returned with the Otoe, having found them 18 miles from the western banks of the Missouri in present-day Nebraska, where they had been engaging in a summer buffalo hunt. Then, about 20 miles north of the present site of Council Bluffs, Iowa (across the Missouri River from Omaha, Nebraska), Lewis and Clark sat down with their first Indians, the Otoe and the Missouri. The Indians were represented by six chiefs, three from each tribe. They brought along a French trader with them to serve as interpreter.

Lewis and Clark, dressed in their formal military uniforms, handed out presents to the Indian leaders, including an American flag, gunpowder, whiskey, various trinkets, and a specially tailored coat for one of the chiefs who could not attend the council. As Clark recorded in his journal, he and Lewis met with the chiefs "to let them Know of the change of Government, The wishes of our Government to Cultivate friendship with them, the Objects of our journy and to present them with a flag and Some Small presents." [20] Clark also wrote in his journal of the tribal leaders who brought along gifts of their own, including "Water millions [watermelons]." [21] As the leaders of the Corps counseled with the Otoe and Missouri chiefs, they told them that the tribes would have to begin trading with the Americans. The meeting went well, and the expedition left the Otoe and Missouri Indians in peace. (A council two weeks later with additional Otoe chiefs did not go well, as one, Little Thief, demanded rifles and ammunition, not trinkets and speeches. He left the council without any of the Corps' guns.)

A week after the successful council with the Otoe and Missouri, near the place where the Great Sioux River runs into the Missouri, Lewis and Clark led a small group on a separate exploration. While exploring, they discovered several important Indian holy sites. Examining these places helped Lewis and Clark understand more about the Indian culture they were beginning to encounter that summer. The small party of corpsmen visited the grave of the Omaha chief Blackbird, who had died of smallpox, along with 400 of his tribe, three years earlier. His grave was a strange one, because the chief had been buried sitting on his horse under a huge earth mound. The Americans honored this chief, who was said to have had magical powers, by hanging an American flag on a nearby tree.

During this leg of the trip, the expedition ate well. There was plenty of game to hunt and, on the northern prairies, the group's hunters killed their first antelope and shot many different kinds of birds. Earlier that month, north of the Little Sioux River, the Corps saw, in Lewis' words, "a great number of feather floating down the river . . . a very extraordinary appearance . . . [covering] sixty or seventy yards of the breadth of the river" for three miles." [22] Upstream, the men "were surprised by . . . a flock of Pillican." [23] They captured a pelican, and, with scientific curiosity, filled the bird's beak with water to see how much it would hold (five gallons). They also saw other strange natural sights, such as a burrowing animal that stood on its hind legs and barked like a small dog. The men called the small creatures

A TENSE ENCOUNTER WITH THE TETON SIOUX

Throughout the 28 months Lewis and Clark crossed the American West, they encountered dozens of Native American tribes. Although most of their encounters were peaceful, a few were tense, featuring an element of violence. One such encounter took place on the Missouri River near modern-day Pierre, South Dakota, and it was the closest the entire expedition came to being completely wiped out.

Late in September 1804, the men of the expedition reached the region of the Teton Sioux, a river tribe Lewis and Clark knew by reputation. The Teton Sioux were notorious on the river, because they "usually stopped upriver trading parties altogether and forced them to dispose of their goods at ruinously low prices which the Sioux themselves set and which amounted to little more than robbery."* Although the men of the Corps of Discovery expected trouble from the Teton Sioux, Lewis and Clark understood how important it was to proclaim to these Indians the power and authority of the United States.

For four days, the men of the Corps of Discovery met with the leaders of the Teton Sioux, whose village numbered perhaps 1,000 residents. During these days, "the two sides talked, exchanged gifts, socialized, demonstrated their power, and tried to intimidate each other."** The meeting was tense. On the first day, as the two wary sides talked to one another, the event "degenerated into a tense standoff with rifles cocked, bows strung, swivel guns loaded."*** The scene was defused when the expedition's leaders offered more presents to the Sioux. Then, on September 25, Lewis and Clark took three Teton chiefs—Black Buffalo, Buffalo Medicine, and one known as the Partisan—to see the Americans' boats. They rowed the chiefs out to give them a closer look at the keelboat, but as Clark tried to return the chiefs to the riverbank, three Teton warriors grabbed the pirogue's towrope and tried to take it. It appears the

"prairie dogs" and spent an afternoon trying to catch one. (The one they captured was later sent back down river in a cage. It was eventually delivered to President Jefferson, who sometimes featured the yipping little critter as a centerpiece at dinners in the Executive Mansion.)

By the end of October 1804, the exploring party had reached

Tetons were accustomed to receiving more gifts—a form of extortion—from French traders who regularly tried to come upriver.

Suddenly, the moment became tense. Clark drew his sword, and Lewis quickly ordered his men "to Stand to their arms."[+] The three keelboat weapons—a small cannon and a pair of swiveling, shotgunlike blunderbusses——were trained on the Indians. Although shots and arrows were not exchanged, it was time for the Corps of Discovery to leave the Teton encampment, having accomplished little and having faced the possibility of extermination by a much larger force than their own.

Clark and the others of his party left the Tetons with a poor opinion of that tribe, and the expedition's co-captain later wrote in his journal, "These are the vilest miscreants of the savage race. Unless these people are reduced to order, by coercive measures, I am ready to pronounce that the citizens of the United States can never enjoy but partially the advantages which the Missouri presents."[++]

It was a singular failure of Lewis and Clark's diplomatic efforts among the Missouri River Indians. Adding to the misfortune of the encounter with the Tetons were the instructions given to Lewis by President Jefferson concerning these important Native American residents of the Missouri River: "On that nation [the Teton Sioux] we wish most particularly to make a friendly impression, because of their immense power, and because we learn they are very desirous of being on the most friendly terms with us."[+++]

---

[*] Quoted in DeVoto, *Journals of Lewis and Clark,* 33.
[**] Quoted in Thorp, *Lewis & Clark,* 48.
[***] Quoted in Thomas Schmidt, *National Geographic Guide to the Lewis & Clark Trail* (Washington, D.C.: National Geographic Society, 2002), 66.
[+] Quoted in Fifer and Soderberg, *Along the Trail,* 75.
[++] Quoted in Schmidt, *Guide to the Lewis & Clark Trail,* 68.
[+++] Ibid.

modern-day North Dakota. They made friends with the Mandan and Minnetaree Indians along the Knife River. Here, Lewis and Clark agreed to make winter camp. The Missouri River would soon be frozen over, keeping the Corps from making any progress up the river. The men built a log fort, which they called Fort Mandan. It included two rows of huts, each hut divided into four rooms. The buildings were finished by Christmas Day, when Lewis and Clark raised the American flag.

During the winter, the expedition leaders talked to Indians and French Canadians in the village about what they should expect upriver when the party would set out again in the spring of 1805. One of these Canadians, a man named Toussaint Charbonneau, agreed to take the expedition upriver. Lewis and Clark, however, were more interested in Charbonneau's wife, a young Shoshone Indian girl named Sacajawea. She had been captured by the Minnetaree Indians five years earlier, when she was only 11 years old. As a Shoshone, she would be able to serve as a guide and interpreter for the Corps, because her people lived to the west, near the Rocky Mountains.

By November, the Missouri River was beginning to freeze and snow was falling. By December, the river was frozen, allowing the Mandan to visit the Americans, who were encamped on the opposite banks of the river. The Corps of Discovery and the Mandan men engaged in a buffalo hunt together, the final one for the year 1804. That winter with the Mandan was one of the most pleasant times for the men of the expedition. The Mandan invited the men into their round earth mounds, which stayed warm during those bitterly cold winter months. (Lewis recorded temperatures at 40 degrees below zero.)

By early April, the expedition had set off up the Missouri again, having built six canoes. They sent the keelboat back down river with the French boatmen, the six temporary enlistees, and their scientific specimens and caged animals, Indian artifacts, and buffalo robes. On April 7, at four o'clock in the morning, the reduced party of Americans, numbering 31 men, Sacajawea, and her two-month-old baby boy, set out up the Missouri. They headed north on the river in the two pirogues and the six newly hewn canoes.

During the summer of 1805, the party progressed upriver across much of modern-day Montana. They saw no Indians during the months from May until August. They continued to experience the usual challenges on the river, including violent

Lewis and Clark added the young Shoshone Indian girl Sacajawea to their exploring party after spending the winter of 1804 at Fort Mandan in modern-day North Dakota. She acted as a guide and helped the Corps of Discovery interact with western Indian tribes. She is seen in this painting, created by Alfred Russell in 1904, guiding the expedition across the Rockies.

windstorms. Grizzly bears were a major problem. Lewis, after having shot a buffalo with his rifle, was chased by a grizzly and had to run into the Missouri River to escape. Some of the bears the Corps encountered were shot with as many as ten rifle balls before collapsing. The men came to fear and dread the great beasts. As Clark wrote in his journal, "I find that the curiossity of our party is pretty well satisfyed with rispect to this anamal." [24]

This leg of the trip included some of the most astonishing scenery for the men of the Corps of Discovery. They passed a part of the Missouri River where very high cliffs rose along the banks. The soft sandstone cliffs were strangely shaped, sometimes appearing to the men like man-made columns and towers. Lewis described the beauty and wonder of the region:

> The water in the course of time in decending from those hills and plains on either side of the river has trickled down the soft sand clifts and woarn it into a thousand grotesque figures, which . . . at a distance are made to represent eligant ranges of lofty freestone buildings . . . in other places . . . we see the remains or ruins of eligant buildings; some collumns standing and almost entire with their pedestals and capitals. . . . As we passed on it seemed as if those seens [scenes] of visionary inchantment would never have and [an] end.[25]

In early June, the expedition members found themselves facing a new problem. At this point in their trip upriver, the Missouri became two rivers. Actually, only one of the rivers was the Missouri. The other was the Marias River, which the Corps was not expecting to find. Lewis and Clark were uncertain which river was the one to follow. The two leaders decided to each take a group of men and explore the two river choices. On June 13, Captain Lewis heard a sound that told him he was on the right river. In the distance, he could finally see a column of mist rising from the river. This was the Great Falls of the Missouri River. Here the river cascaded down an 80-foot drop along a bluff nearly 1,000 feet long. Lewis sent a man back to Clark to tell him of this discovery.

When Clark caught up with Lewis, the co-captains and their men faced a daunting task. They would have to portage, or carry, their supplies and their canoes around the falls. The men built crude carts from cottonwood trees to haul their loads. It took the men 24 days to get the entire party and its equipment and stores around the cascading waterfalls of the Missouri. The carts the men cobbled together did not perform well, because the "axles or tongues on the wheels broke three times and had to be repaired."[26] The work was grueling and exhausting, and the men struggled against the summer heat, their feet cut deeply by extensive outcroppings of prickly pear cactus. The calendar would show mid-July before this difficult task was completed.

A week later, on July 22, the party reached the Three Forks of the Missouri, where three rivers formed the headwaters of the great western waterway. The co-captains named the rivers after important political leaders back in Washington: the Jefferson, the Madison (Jefferson's secretary of state), and the Gallatin (the secretary of the treasury).

By arriving at the Three Forks, the Lewis and Clark expedition accomplished a feat no American party had before. They had paddled the entire length of the Missouri from its mouth in modern-day Missouri to the eastern reaches of the Rocky Mountains in western Montana. Their expedition would continue to take them west, away from the river, over the following year (the party remained along the Pacific Coast though the winter of 1805–6) and they would return to the Missouri River to make their way downstream, back to St. Louis and their American homes in September 1806.

The Missouri River had been a great western mystery to the Corps of Discovery in 1804, but they had covered every mile; charted and mapped its course; established relations with the Indians who lived along its banks; collected its flora and fauna; noted its volatility, its wildness, and its unpredictable nature; and opened the way for future generations of Americans as they moved into the west of the Great Plains. Even as the Corps made its way down the Missouri that summer of 1806, they met the first vanguard of American entrepreneurs coming upriver— fur trappers and traders and the mountain men that soon became part of the legend of the West and of the history of the Missouri River.

4

An Empire of Fur

Although the expedition of Meriwether Lewis and William Clark helped open the Great Far West to American fur trade, it was not America's first experience with such a commodity. From the founding of colonial America in the early seventeenth century and for nearly three centuries to follow, "fur trading was a principal commercial enterprise of the frontier."[27] As a new generation of Americans looked toward the vast region of the Louisiana Territory, they saw great potential for yet another fur-related trade, this one in beaver pelts. They looked to the Missouri River as their ticket into the world of icy mountain streams where the beaver lived in abundance. As one historian has stated it, "The Missouri River was the only natural highway to and from the West. In a geographic sense, it was ideally situated to handle the fur business."[28] William Clark himself had noted the value of the Missouri River: "We view this passage [the Missouri] across the continent as affording immence advantages to the fir trade."[29]

To the fur traders of the early nineteenth century, beaver skins were equivalent to "fur gold." Many of the traders left the hard work of trapping beaver to the rugged mountain men and the Indians who populated the Rocky Mountain region where beaver were so plentiful. Traders knew the value of beaver fur, however, and made shrewd deals to get the skins to eastern American and European markets. Even as Lewis and Clark led their party up the Missouri, western beaver skins were selling for $180 per 100 pounds. A prime, unblemished, large beaver skin, with its thick, soft, luxurious fur, could measure larger than two feet square and bring a price of $6 to $8. A skilled mountain man who trapped the western streams for a season could anticipate collecting 120 beaver pelts, a harvest worth the then-princely sum of $1,000. As long as the demand for fur remained high, thousands of intrepid westerners would risk their lives to make their fortunes in the fur business.

As American traders prepared to launch up the Missouri River to engage in western beaver trapping, they introduced a boat called a Mackinaw to the Missouri. The typical Mackinaw was

In the early nineteenth century, beaver skins became known as "fur gold" because of their high value. Because of its location the Missouri was the ideal route for the fur trade and thousands of traders risked their lives to engage in beaver trapping on the Missouri and hopefully make their fortune. This painting by Karl Bodmer shows beavers in their natural habitat on the river.

flat-bottomed, an essential part of its design considering the shallowness of the Missouri and the constant threat of sandbars. Its prow and stern were streamlined. An average Mackinaw measured 40 feet in length and 10 feet at its widest point, or beam. The boat featured a rudder at its stern and could be poled or paddled upstream. Such boats drew little water and were fashioned out of the cottonwood forests found along the banks of the middle leg of the Missouri's lengthy course. An additional incentive to the use of the Mackinaw was its lack of expense. A Mackinaw could be hired, complete with crew, by a river trader to haul 15 tons of freight for as little as $2 a day.

The Mackinaw was serviceable on the Missouri, and another popular watercraft was the keelboat. Lewis and Clark had proven the viability of keelboats on the Missouri, and the early fur trappers and traders liked them because they could carry a large number of furs plus much additional cargo and supplies. Although keelboats were more expensive than Mackinaws, they could make the voyage upriver as well as down, lasted longer than Mackinaws, and could carry heavier loads.

Just as Lewis and Clark's men had struggled taking their 55-foot-long keelboat up the Missouri, so did the fur men. Many of the later models were larger than the Corps of Discovery's, measuring up to 70 feet in length, and they were unwieldy, heavy boats. As one Missouri River traveler, a British botanist named John Bradbury, noted during a keelboat trip upriver in 1811, "At every sudden turn the momentum of the boats had a continual tendency to throw them ashore on the outer bank, which it required all the skill of the steersman, and the strength of the oarsmen, to prevent. In two instances we were very near being carried into the woods, in places where the river overflowed its banks." [30] Whether on a Mackinaw or a keelboat, traveling up the Missouri was a difficult proposition. The progress was, on most days, so slow that a person walking along the bank of the river could move up the river faster than those struggling against the Missouri's untamed corridor.

During the half-century after the Lewis and Clark expedition, American entrepreneurs developed an extensive fur trading system on the Upper Missouri River. One of the earliest American efforts was launched by John Jacob Astor, a German immigrant to the United States. In 1808, President Jefferson wrote a letter to Meriwether Lewis, then governor of Upper Louisiana, of Astor's early efforts to establish an American fur trade system on the Missouri River: "A powerful company is at length forming for taking up the Indian trade on a large scale. It will be under the direction of a most excellent man, a Mr. Astor, merchant of New York, long engaged in the business and the perfect master of it." [31] Astor's name for his new capitalist venture based in fur was

RUN FOR YOUR LIFE, JOHN COLTER

More than one of the men who accompanied Lewis and Clark west in 1804–6 remained in the West after the expedition returned to St. Louis. One of those who chose to remain in the open environs of Upper Louisiana was John Colter. In time, his adventures became the stuff of fur-era legend.

Colter became involved in the fur trade as a trapper even before the Lewis and Clark expedition was completed. While the Corps of Discovery was returning down the Missouri River from two years of exploring, it was met by fur traders going upriver. After talking with some of the intrepid traders and rivermen, Colter requested permission from the captains to leave the Corps and join those headed west. Permission was granted.

In just a few years, Colter was employed by the American Fur Company, working for Manuel Lisa. During the trapping season of 1809, Colter was part of a group of trappers and traders sent to the headwaters of the Missouri River. He and his comrades discovered the region to be teeming with beaver, and Colter soon faced one of the most deadly challenges of his life.

While out one morning trapping with an associate named Potts, Colter was surprised by a party of Blackfoot Indians, who killed his comrade on the spot. When Colter was taken captive and showed his "extreme bravery,"* the Blackfoot gave him an opportunity to save himself. According to the story told later by Colter, the Blackfoot asked him how fast he could run. Colter wisely told them he ran "like a crippled bird."** When he convinced the Blackfoot warriors he was telling the truth, they stripped him naked and gave him a head start. They intended to chase him down and kill him.

Given just seconds to put distance between himself and his captors, Colter

"the American Fur Company." The company was an unparalleled success. When Astor retired in 1834, he was one of the richest men in America and his company "reached westward from its impressive Great Lakes depot on Mackinac Island, to crude subposts well beyond the confluence of the Missouri and Yellowstone rivers."[32] Part of Astor's success (he did not go west himself but rather operated his fur empire from New York City) was his ability to employ the best traders in the western fur business. Such men as Auguste and Pierre Choteau, Pierre dashed ahead, "ignoring the prickle pear and rocks that must have dug into his feet—exerting himself so hard that according to him blood began to gush from his nose and to cover his face."*** The fast-moving fur trapper outran all his would-be assailants except one, whom Colter turned and subdued with the warrior's own spear. Colter took to his heels again until he reached the Missouri River. Diving in, he hid among some driftwood for the remainder of the day as hundreds of Blackfoot Indians searched for him, frequently submerging himself completely underwater and breathing through a hollow reed.

That night, the exhausted, naked, bleeding mountain man began to walk to safety. For more than a week, Colter pushed through the wilderness of western Montana until he reached a trading post on the Bighorn River, one newly built by Manuel Lisa, his boss. As incredible as Colter's story was, it managed to make him a western legend.

Colter's former Corps of Discovery comrade, George Drouillard, had his own unfortunate encounter with the Blackfoot the following year. In the spring of 1810, Drouillard was working as a trapper for Lisa when a Blackfoot party came on him and killed him. When his body was later found, just two miles from a trading post, it was discovered "mangled in a horrible manner, his head cut off, his entrails torn out and his body hacked to pieces."+

---

  * Quoted in Gildart, *Montana's Missouri River*, 21.

  ** Ibid.

  *** Ibid.

  + Quoted in O'Neil, *The Rivermen*, 64.

Menard, Andrew Henry, and Manuel Lisa were only a handful of Astor's agents who "sent their trappers up the Missouri into the Dakotas where they secured a rich harvest."[33]

Manuel Lisa proved to be one of the great field agents of the nineteenth-century American fur era. Lisa had first entered the western fur trade in 1806, the year Lewis and Clark returned from their epic expedition. Lisa's company, the Missouri Fur Company, was one of the first organized for the trade on the Upper Missouri River. His chief of operations, George Drouillard, had participated in the Lewis and Clark expedition. Both Drouillard and another of Lewis and Clark's men, John Colter, were among the first to trek up the Missouri, beyond the Yellowstone confluence to the mouth of the Bighorn River to establish fur trade connections with the local Crow Indians. At the Yellowstone–Missouri Confluence, Manuel Lisa ordered the construction of the first American fur-trading post in the Far West. It went by two names: Lisa's Fort or Fort Manuel.

After the construction of the fort, Lisa returned to St. Louis, the Mississippi River town that had long been an important outpost for French trading efforts on the Missouri River. In the spring of 1809, Lisa gathered 350 men to proceed up the Missouri in a fleet of 13 keelboats and barges "with the intention of expanding trading and trapping in the most dangerous of all areas—the hostile Blackfeet country near the upper three forks of the Missouri."[34] At Three Forks, John Colter, employed by Lisa, directed the construction of another fort.

The region of the headwaters of the Missouri was prime beaver country, but although the work of trapping beaver, setting the traps in cold mountain streams, and working in buckskin clothes that remain wet constantly could be rewarding financially, the odds of surviving a trapping season on the Missouri River and its tributaries were poor. These men died of exposure and starvation, froze to death, and were killed by Indians, especially the Blackfoot. Of the men Lisa dispatched to trap beaver in 1809, perhaps as many as 30 were killed by Indians. As for Lisa, he remained involved in the western Missouri River fur trade until 1820. He died at the age of 47.

Manuel Lisa left an indelible mark on the Missouri River fur trade, and others made similar contributions. In 1828, Kenneth McKenzie turned his eye to the Upper Missouri beaver trade. McKenzie, described by one historian as "the ablest leader that the American Fur Company ever possessed,"[35] built one of the most important fur trading posts on the Missouri, near its confluence with the Yellowstone, and called his outpost Fort Union. The outpost became the jewel of a fur company called the Upper Missouri Outfit, which was formed earlier in the 1820s when two companies, including Astor's American Fur Company, joined together to cooperate in the region's fur business.

Fort Union, when completed in 1830, represented one of the most important cornerstones of the western upriver fur trade. It was built at a site that Lewis and Clark had suggested 25 years earlier as strategic. For 30 years, Fort Union dominated the beaver and bison robe trade of Montana and the Dakotas, because "the Missouri–Yellowstone system was ideally suited for transporting men, furs, buffalo robes, and supplies up or down the rivers." [36] The fort was built on the north bank of the Missouri, six miles from the mouth of the Yellowstone, about 60 feet from the river bank. Its presence on the river gave it a commanding dominance of the "sprawling prairie that gave way on the west and north to rolling hills and bluffs." [37] Although it was called a fort, its primary purpose was to serve as a trading complex, not as a military outpost, although it was designed to provide defense in the case of Indian attack. The construction was on the *poteaux-en-terre*, or "post-in-ground," method, involving cottonwood tree trunks set vertically into the ground. Inside the fort were bastions that served as "watchtowers, storage rooms for armaments and ordnance . . . and they also offered pleasant vantage points from which to enjoy the sweeping panoramic view or a cool evening breeze." [38] Blockhouses dominated two of the fort's opposite corners. The adjacent grounds also hosted an icehouse measuring 24 by 21 feet, which was "well filled with ice during the winter, which supply generally last[ed] till fall." [39] The icehouse was used to store and keep the post's supply of fresh meat. (The original Fort Union was only used for three years; it burned down in 1833 and was replaced by a second post that was much larger and more complex. Fort Union II measured 237 feet by 245 feet.)

Fort Union soon became the center of a distinctive world inhabited by St. Louis merchants, grizzled mountain men, veteran rivermen, and Indians representing a half-dozen major northern Great Plains tribes. From the beginning, Fort Union was considered unique, the result of an intended long-term vision for western trade and commerce. As the historian Barton Barbour explains,

> Fort Union was much more than a squalid and ephemeral place where shoddy goods were traded for furs over a few years, only to be carelessly abandoned. Instead, it was calculated to convey the impression of power, solidity, and permanence. Its owners meant it to be a magnet for customers and a grand stage on which to perform the trade ritual, even under conditions that demanded high security. The post provided housing and workplaces for a diverse community, isolated and exposed, in the Upper Missouri "wilderness."[40]

By the spring of 1830, McKenzie had moved into Fort Union, and the new facility served as the base for approximately 120 engagés, or fur trappers, employed by McKenzie's company, nearly half of the number working for the Upper Missouri Outfit. Soon, McKenzie was well-known along the river, and his company became extremely profitable. He became known as "King of the Upper Missouri" or "King McKenzie." It was a title the Scottish immigrant tried to live up to. At Fort Union, he lived in a lavish style for one stationed in the Upper Missouri frontier. Historian R.C. Gildart described the image McKenzie projected:

> McKenzie played the part. He dressed for dinner at a table set with china and silverware. His subordinates sat at the long table in descending order of importance. Meat, vegetable, dairy products, and good bread were served at his table, with coffee, tea, and wine. The ordinary laborers, sitting at a separate table, also ate plentifully, but of a restricted fare.[41]

Fort Union was an important building block in McKenzie's plans to establish an Upper Missouri trade system, but it was only part of his plan. The focus of McKenzie's fur trading efforts was to develop the trade farther upriver with the Blackfoot Indians. He dispatched his agents, including a former employee of the

British Hudson Bay Company who spoke Blackfoot, to the Upper Missouri, with a large supply of gifts and "a promise to build a trading house for the Blackfeet in their own country." [42] When negotiations proved successful, McKenzie ordered two dozen men into the Upper Missouri region with instructions to build Fort Piegan at the confluence of the Marias and Missouri Rivers. Through the first season, the trade at Piegan was brisk, as the Blackfoot delivered many furs for exchange. That spring, however, after McKenzie's men loaded up their furs and slipped downriver to Fort Union, the Blackfoot burned Fort Piegan.

Just three years later, another McKenzie agent, D. D. Mitchell, was ordered into the Marias–Missouri region. He elected to build his post near the site of Fort Piegan, along the Marias. The Blackfoot in the region seemed restless that year, and the men sent to build the new trading post remained on their keelboat at night, posting constant guards. In the meantime, Mitchell spent much time negotiating with the Blackfoot leaders, trying to keep them pacified long enough to work out trade agreements. When the fort was completed, it was dubbed "Fort McKenzie."

The fort was used for the Upper Missouri fur trade for the next 10 years. It proved to be a successful extension of the fur trade, and the Blackfoot traded at its gates extensively. In 1841 alone, Blackfoot hunters delivered 21,000 buffalo robes to the fort. For the Upper Missouri Outfit's parent company, the American Fur Company, it became the linchpin to continued success on the upper river. The hegemony of Fort McKenzie was cut short, however, when a new superintendent, Francis A. Chardon, arrived in the early 1840s. Chardon was described by one historian as "a hotheaded Frenchman who bartered liquor freely, befriended the wrong people, and left a trail of tension from post to post." [43] After one of Chardon's fur agents was killed by a Blackfoot Indian, the fort's commander ordered the massacre of the next group of Blackfoot warriors that showed up at Fort McKenzie. The plot was a poor decision of itself, and when Chardon's men killed an arriving Piegan Indian band by mistake, the error was compounded even more. The massacre

Fort Union was completed in 1830 as a cornerstone of the fur trade on the Upper Missouri and a building block in the establishment of an Upper Missouri trade system. Unfortunately, the success of the fur trade started to decline in the 1840s, and Fort Union was moved upstream to its present location north of the Montana–North Dakota border, seen here.

was a serious blow to Fort McKenzie's future. The Blackfoot did not return to the post.

In an effort to lure back the business of the Blackfoot, Chardon arranged for the construction of a new fur post, one downstream at the confluence of the Missouri and Judith Rivers, where his men built Fort Chardon. The American Fur Company soon replaced Chardon with another agent, Alexander Culbertson, who had his work of diplomatically drawing back the Blackfoot trade cut out for him. Culbertson first destroyed the fort named for the man responsible for the break in the fur company's relations with Montana river region tribes and built another 12 miles downriver from modern-day Fort Benton. The new post was called Fort Lewis, after Captain Meriwether Lewis. (Records show that the fort also went by additional names, including Fort Henry, Fort Honore Picotte, and the Fort of the Blackfeet.)

Fort Lewis did not prove successful, however. It had been built several miles from any significant stand of river trees, which Indians needed to hack out canoes and cross the river from the north. Culbertson ordered Fort Lewis dismantled in 1847 and rebuilt three miles downriver. The new site was also called Fort Lewis for a while, but by 1848, it was renamed Fort Benton, after a senator from Missouri who was a strong supporter of the western fur trade.

As for McKenzie himself, he served as the director of the Upper Missouri Outfit until 1834, running the business of the company's trade and hosting several important guests to the Upper Missouri region, including the renowned naturalist-painter, John James Audubon. During the short time McKenzie was involved in the Upper Missouri trade, he accumulated personal profits of $150,000, a princely sum in that day. However, the heyday of the western fur trade could not last forever. By the 1840s, the trade was in decline. Silk fashion was replacing the fur craze, yet the fort remained a center of trade on the Missouri River until it was torn down in 1867. Old Fort Union was then hauled upstream to a site just over the modern-day North Dakota–Montana border and reassembled as a military post, renamed Fort Buford.

5

"Fire Canoes"

For hundreds, perhaps thousands of years, countless river travelers had plied their courses along the Missouri River in muscle-powered boats such as bullboats, dugouts, and canoes. The early nineteenth century brought a new type of watercraft to the river: boats powered by steam. Steamboats were introduced to the western rivers of early America in 1811. The first western steamer was built in Pittsburgh, Pennsylvania and piloted down the Ohio and Mississippi Rivers by its inventor, Nicholas Roosevelt. Within a few years, dozens of small, underpowered, one-deck steamboats were paddling up and down the two rivers between Louisville, Kentucky, and the port of New Orleans. These early Mississippi–Ohio steamboats were successful as carriers of American trade, commerce, and river passengers, and the Missouri did not have to wait long for its own.

In 1819, the Missouri River had its first. That year, Captain John Nelson "accepted a charter paid for by St. Louis merchants and civic leaders to take his boat, the *Independence,* up the Missouri River to the vicinity of the Chariton River"[44] Nelson's cargo included flour, whiskey, sugar, and iron, as well as several important citizens of St. Louis. The first steamer on the river, powered by a low-condensing engine, struggled against the Missouri's wild current, taking 13 days to cover 150 miles on the river. The average keelboat of the day usually took fewer days to cover the same stretch of river. When the *Independence* steamed to the landing at Franklin, Missouri, the whole town turned out in celebration. An entire day of feasting followed. Almost two dozen toasts were raised in honor of Captain Nelson's successful trip upriver, including one to the Missouri River itself: "Its last wave will roll the abundant tribute of our region to the Mexican gulf, in reference to the auspices of this day."[45] Everyone believed that the coming of the steamboat to the longest river in America, the great artery into the western interior, would change the river dramatically and all who lived along its banks. They could not have been more correct.

Other Missouri River steamers followed in rapid succession. The second was the *Western Engineer,* one of a small fleet of

The steamboat era was introduced to the Missouri River in 1819, and steamboats were the principal transportation for trade, commerce, and passengers throughout the rest of the century. The *Rosebud*, seen here in an 1878 photograph, was an historic Missouri riverboat that traveled from Bismarck, North Dakota to Montana.

western steamboats built under a contract with the United States government. In 1819, the U.S. secretary of war, South Carolinian John C. Calhoun, ordered the forming of a fleet of six steamboats up the Missouri River to its confluence with the Yellowstone. He wanted to see the construction of an American fort there "to deter British incursions into American territory." [46] The contract for five of the steamboats was given to an unscrupulous Ohio River steamboat operator named James Johnson. Through government friends and connections, Johnson was able to charge an inflated price for his steamboats, which included the *Thomas Jefferson, Expedition, R. M. Johnson, J. C. Calhoun,*

STEAMBOATS DELIVER SMALLPOX TO THE RIVER

Non-Indian fur trappers, traders, and mountain men generally risked their lives in search of beaver in the cold, highland streams of Rocky Mountain Indian country, and they also delivered a form of death to the Indians they encountered: smallpox. The western fur traders delivered the deadly disease up the Missouri River in the early 1800s. A non-Indian with smallpox might die from the illness, but many also survived, often scarred for life from the aftereffects of the sores, or pox, that spread over the skin. For Indians, who had no natural immunity to the disease, the result was frequently a difficult death. It was only one deadly disease introduced to the Indians—others included cholera, influenza, and even measles—but smallpox was easily spread, and the results were often devastating and tragic.

One of the most severe outbreaks of smallpox on the Missouri River during the days of the fur trade took place in 1837. That summer, the *St. Peters,* a steamboat owned by the Missouri Fur Company, arrived at Fort Union, near the confluence of the Missouri and Yellowstone Rivers. Onboard, several passengers, including some Indian women, were dying of smallpox. The disease began to spread through the fort. Soon, "people at the fort fell into utter panic, all fearing for their lives."[*] In a desperate effort to halt the spread of the disease, the superintendent of the fort, Charles Larpenteur, tried to inoculate people. Since the early 1700s, European doctors had been inoculating humans by scratching an arm with a needle exposed to cowpox, a similar but much less deadly disease, which rendered the recipient immune to smallpox. With scanty medical knowledge, Larpenteur rubbed the pus from a smallpox victim's sores into cuts he made on the arms of healthy people. Sadly, in his ignorance, he merely succeeded in transferring the disease to new victims. Before the outbreak ran its course, 27 people died at Fort Union. In the middle of the contagion's run, several hundred Assiniboine Indians arrived at the fort to trade, spreading the disease farther.

The disease struck elsewhere on the river that summer, including at Fort McKenzie, where many Blackfoot were exposed. How many Indians died of smallpox that summer is not known, but the record estimates that at least 800 Assiniboine and as many as 700 Blackfoot died. Downriver, the Mandan and Hidatsa also died in large numbers. The Mandan were "virtually annihilated."[**] Some estimates calculate the number of Indians killed during the 1837 Missouri River outbreak at 15,000.

[*] Quoted in Barbour, *Fort Union,* 136.

[**] Ibid., 138.

and *Exchange*. All five of the boats were of inferior quality. A separate contract was issued for a sixth boat, the *Western Engineer*. Its design was strange indeed, its "upper works built to resemble a scaly serpent that would emit steam through its nostrils and thus frighten off any Indians who might be inclined to hostility."[47]

The six steamers were dispatched up the Missouri in late June 1819. The timing was poor, because the river was near its peak from the western mountain thaw and spring rise. All five of Johnson's boats proved ill-suited for the rapid currents of the Missouri River, having been designed for a deeper river. The farthest any of Johnson's boats were able to reach was the confluence of the Kansas and Missouri Rivers, after struggling several hundred miles upstream. (One of the five, the *J. C. Calhoun*, never even made it to the Missouri, having burned a hole in its boiler while still on the Mississippi.)

The *Western Engineer* proved much more successful. Her captain had taken her up the Missouri a few weeks earlier, having left St. Louis on June 9, and none of Johnson's boats ever caught up with her, even after the *Western Engineer* ran aground twice and stopped at Franklin, Missouri, for a week. On August 1, the *Western Engineer* reached Fort Osage, just east of modern-day Kansas City, Missouri. On September 17, the hard-working steamer reached the site where Lewis and Clark had met with the Otoe Indians in the summer of 1804 (near Council Bluffs, Iowa). The *Western Engineer* had managed to cover 1,100 miles of the Missouri River, but proceeding farther was out of the question. Even the underpowered stern-wheeler could not possibly complete the remaining 800 miles to the Yellowstone River's confluence. Disappointed all around, Congress gave up on the project.

Despite their limitations, these chugging, smoke-belching steamboats "embodied all the fears and frustrations linked to the white man's presence" for the Indians.[48] A common Indian name given the steam-powered boats was "fire canoes." In the early days of steamboating on the Missouri, some Indians became so fearful at the approach of a steamboat that they "shot their horses and dogs to appease the Great Spirit."[49] Because the steamboats' smokestacks emitted great plumes of thick, black smoke and their engines produced eerie mechanical noises, the Indians believed that the paddle wheelers were living beings with minds of their own. As one Indian observer noted, "It sees its way and takes the deep water in the middle of the channel." [50]

The riverboats that plied up and down the Missouri in the early days of steamers were typically low-key structures, measuring between 100 and 130 feet in length. They drew between three and five feet of water and pushed up the river with underpowered engines at speeds rarely faster than six miles an hour. (Later steamboat models were designed even flatter, some drawing as little as 14 inches of water. During low water stages, when the Missouri River ran no more than waist-deep in places, the flatter the steamboat bottom, the better.)

Such early Missouri steamboats boasted only one engine, situated on the boat's single deck, called the boiler deck, usually near the bow of the craft. The only structure above the deck was the pilothouse and the single chimney of earlier models. The main shaft, which connected the engine with the boat's paddle wheel, was exposed, running along most of the boat's length.

One singular problem steamboat men on the Missouri River faced was the mud content of the water. Because the steamers used river water in their boilers and "a cubic foot of brown liquid from the Missouri could contain handfuls of silt and sand," [51] steamboat boilers quickly filled with the gooey river muck. After just a day of paddling on the Big Muddy, the steamboat crew often shut down the boat's boilers, drained the boiler and then shoveled the mud from the paddle wheeler's engine. If the mud in a boiler was left unattended, it could cause the engine's valves and pistons to wear out and grind to a halt.

Piloting a steamboat on the Missouri River, given the river's unpredictability, its shifting course, and its watery path thick with sandbars, snags, and other underwater obstacles, was always difficult work. Steamboat pilots had to memorize the river and become familiar with its hazards. For those times when the river was low and the hazards multiplied, the skilled river

The Missouri River was often known as "Big Muddy" because its waters were so murky and silt-laden. This photograph of the river in North Dakota shows the thick mud ripples on its riverbank.

pilots used a variety of techniques to even the odds that their boats would navigate the Big Muddy successfully.

When a boat became immobilized on a sandbar, a process called "grasshoppering" was used, which involved a pair of lengthy poles or spars on the bow of the boat that were lowered into the river bottom at a 45-degree angle. Ropes or cables were attached to the spars and then to a capstan, and the boat was winched forward, off the sandbar, as the spars gave the boat a forward leverage. To negotiate upstream against rapids, a steamboat crew might drive a large timber, called a "deadman," on the river bank and rig up a rope and pulley system to the timber and pull the boat slowly through the whitewater and upriver.

When the Missouri was at a low level, pilots sometimes engaged their steamers in "double tripping." To lighten a boat's load and allow the steamer to draw less water, the cargo was offloaded and the passengers were delivered to their destinations. The steamer then returned to pick up the cargo, making a second run of at least part of the river voyage. This technique was common on the Upper Missouri as steamboats plied their way to Fort Benton. During one low-water year—1869—three out of every four steamers unloaded their cargoes 10 miles downstream at Dauphin's Rapids and delivered their passengers and cargo in two separate runs.

Although the steamboats of the nineteenth century improved the state of river traffic on the Missouri, the boats had a singular ecological impact on the river. Because the boats burned wood, steamer crews constantly felled cottonwood trees for fuel. The amount of wood cut, resulting in trees removed, was astonishing. A steamer making the upriver trip from St. Louis to Fort Benton might consume as many as 30 cords of wood a day, and the river voyage could take more than two months. Because hundreds of riverboats plied the Missouri River waters by the 1860s, the amount of wood cut for fuel led to the destruction of countless cottonwood groves along the Big Muddy.

Within a generation of the first steamboats reaching the Missouri, the basic design had undergone an extensive change. The later models featured at least two decks, with the pilothouse still perched above the boat's top deck. Multiple engines were launched on the Missouri, and a variety of safety features, including whistles and steam valves and gauges to let the engineers onboard know the level of steam pressure in the boat's boilers, were developed. By 1859, approximately 100 steamers were using the Missouri River as a highway of western trade and to bring new settlement to the American West. Even as the Upper Missouri fur trade finally ran its course, by the 1850s and 1860s, the region was littered with mining camps where thousands of gold seekers relied on the steamboats to keep them supplied with foodstuffs and mining equipment, while delivering new miners to the region.

Most of the first generation of riverboat traffic on the Missouri was associated with the fur trade, but by the mid-1850s, despite the untamed nature of the river, regular packet steamer service had arrived on the Big Muddy. During the summer of 1856, through a combination of rail and river steamer, the Pacific Railroad Packet Company was established. Known popularly as the Lightning Line, the company provided steamboat service on the Missouri, completing regularly scheduled runs on the river from one Pacific Railroad town to the next. The company's founder, Captain Barton Able, began his steam packet service with three boats that landed three times weekly at such sites as the Missouri River town of Jefferson City, Missouri's capital. With the steamers connecting passengers and western travelers with regional rail service, the "dual mode of transportation . . . cut hours off travel time."[52] By 1858, Able's fleet had increased to six steamers and had gained the government contract to deliver mail, as well as government freight and supplies. The Lightning Line enjoyed a short run, however, becoming obsolete after just a few years as railroads connected additional western towns to one another, eliminating the need for the steamboat packet service.

During these same years, a packet service called the St. Louis and St. Joseph Union Packet Line was established with a dozen paddle wheelers, but business was never extensive and the company soon closed, having lost money. Other packets, as well as nonscheduled riverboat traffic on the Missouri, increased despite such losses. The year 1859 witnessed 60 steamboats plying the waters of the Missouri River between St. Louis and Sioux City, Iowa.

By the 1860s, the heyday of the Missouri River steamboats was about to end. Although packet steamboating continued on the river until the 1880s, the years between 1840 and 1860 on the Missouri River were the busiest for steamboat traffic. Steamboating on the Missouri had always been a dangerous business, and with the coming of the Civil War, a new dimension of danger was added. Across the state of Missouri, Confederate guerrilla bands targeted Missouri steamers, firing on them and even boarding several. In addition, many of the Missouri paddle wheelers were pressed into duty by the federal government for use transporting supplies and soldiers on the Mississippi, Tennessee, and Cumberland Rivers. Through continuous and difficult wartime use, many of the Missouri steamers simply wore out.

Immediately after the Civil War, new packet lines were established, including the St. Louis and Miami Packet Company, running between St. Louis and Miami, Missouri. The line was successful initially and was lengthened to include packet runs to Lexington and Kansas City, Missouri. In the late 1870s, the company experienced a restructuring and was renamed as the Kansas City Packet Company. The company remained on the river until the late 1880s.

Much of the era of packet steamers took place on the Lower Missouri, but there were intrepid businessmen who formed such companies on the Upper Missouri. Several were contracted by the U.S. government to deliver mail, passengers, and supplies to western mining camps and upriver towns. One, operated by Captain William J. Lountz of Pittsburgh, ran steamers on the Upper River above Bismarck, North Dakota. As the western fur trade petered out, however, so did the profits generated by such Upper Missouri companies.

Yet another nail in the coffin of Missouri steam boating was the advance of the railroads west of the Mississippi River. During the 1860s and 1870s, rail lines stretched across Missouri, Iowa, and Nebraska. Individual lines ran from the Missouri towns of Hannibal and St. Louis to St. Joseph and Kansas City, respectively. Others ran from the Mississippi river town of Dubuque, Iowa, to Council Bluffs. Such railroads took business away from the steamboats specifically and the river in general.

Some river entrepreneurs were not prepared to give up on the viability of steamboats on the Missouri, however. In 1879, several investors tried to keep packet boating alive on the Big Muddy, forming a company and building three new Missouri

CAPTURING THE RIVER ON CANVAS

During the decades after the Lewis and Clark Expedition, most of the non-Indians who traveled up the Missouri River were involved in the fur trade. Some of those who ventured up the river, however, were intent on exploring another facet of the river altogether. Just one year after Fort McKenzie opened for business, two unique visitors reached the fur-trading outpost. One was a German prince named Alexander Phillip Maximilian of Wied-Neuwied. The other was Karl Bodmer, a Swiss artist who accompanied Prince Maximilian.

Prince Maximilian, a veteran of the Napoleonic Wars, was a naturalist, intent on visiting the Upper Missouri and the American West to study the western Native Americans. He had already completed expeditions in the jungles of Brazil where he studied native cultures and natural history. Maximilian and Bodmer sailed from Europe, trekked across the eastern United States, and met with William Clark in St. Louis before taking passage on a keelboat up the Missouri River. Along the river, the two European partners observed Indians, usually in the vicinity of fur-trading posts, as well as in their own village settings.

It was Bodmer's task to produce artworks documenting the sights he and the prince encountered on their unique study trip. The Swiss painter rendered several wonderful re-creations of life on the great river, including mountain men in their Mackinaws, Indians making a winter crossing on a frozen Missouri, and an encounter with grizzly bears. During the late summer of 1833, Bodmer and Maximilian were eyewitnesses to a battle among Assiniboine, Cree, and Piegan warriors, which Bodmer later produced on canvas. Such renderings remain a collection depicting a single, unique era in the history of the Missouri and its early

steamers: *Dacotah, Wyoming,* and *Montana.* The steamers were designed to successfully navigate the entire length of the Missouri from its Mississippi River mouth to Fort Benton, Montana. For a while, the boats were a success. The *Dacotah* completed seven trips up the Missouri throughout the 1880s, carrying hundreds of tons of cargo. On one river trip, the *Dacotah* returned with a record-breaking load of cargo that included "16,000 sacks of wheat and 5,000 pieces of freight."[53] In 1882, the *Wyoming* delivered a cargo from Fort Benton that included more than 300 head of livestock, a record for any nineteenth-century steamboat. The *Montana's* history on the river was cut short after only nineteenth-century inhabitants. During the months of his Missouri River visit, Bodmer produced "nearly 250 images, [while] the prince had filled several notebooks and they had sent many crates to Europe packed with botanical, ethnological, and zoological specimens."*

Bodmer was only one of the noted artists of the period to produce paintings of Native American life on the Missouri River during the 1830s. George Catlin, an American painter from the East Coast, went west on the Missouri River in 1832 as a passenger on the American Fur Company's first steamboat, the *Yellowstone*. Catlin was intent on documenting the Native American life on the Missouri River. During his first expedition west, Catlin produced 170 paintings and watercolors depicting Indian life, as well as portraits of important Indian chiefs. He worked quickly on many of his paintings, "sometimes whipping out as many as six finely detailed works in a single day."** Between 1832 and 1837, Catlin made three trips to the West, producing paintings depicting life among Missouri River tribes, including the Mandan, Lakota, Blackfoot, Osage, Crow, Piegan, Assiniboine, Cree, Otoe, Kansas, Omaha, Arikara, and others.

Catlin's contribution to documenting the cultural history of these tribes remains invaluable. His works depict a way of life that barely survived his third trip to the western Missouri River region. By 1837, many of these great Missouri River tribes had experienced extensive outbreaks of smallpox, which virtually wiped out their existence.

* Quoted in Barbour, *Fort Union,* 81.
** Quoted in Keith Wheeler, *The Chroniclers* (New York: TIME-LIFE Books, 1976), 102.

two trips on the Upper Missouri, when a tornado damaged her in Bismarck, North Dakota.

Despite the greater trends away from steamboating on the Missouri River during the final decades of the nineteenth century, some companies fought to remain in business on the river. From 1879 to 1890, the Benton Line ran the river, followed by the St. Louis and Rocheport Packet Company, which ran from 1891 until 1894. Among the last of the Missouri steamboat packet companies were the Kansas City and Missouri River Transportation Company (1891–1909) and the Hermann Packet Company (1901–1909).

6

Taming the Missouri

Throughout the steamboat era of the nineteenth century, the Missouri experienced some of its most drastic changes. The river witnessed the growth of its non-Indian settlements and towns, as well as the development of a Missouri economy based on more than just the trading of furs between whites and Indians. As the river became a more productive highway of migration and trade, significant steps were taken to change not only how the river was utilized but also the nature of the river itself. For thousands of years, the Missouri had remained a river that knew no boundaries. Its wildness ensured that all who plied its waters did so with an element of risk. Submerged trees—some weighing many tons—lay beneath the murky waters of the Missouri, ripping through the bottoms of many of the river's nineteenth-century steamboats. Of the 700 steamboats that paddled up and down the Missouri River, nearly 300 were destroyed by tree snags and other river obstacles between 1830 and 1902. One estimate suggests that perhaps as many as 70 percent of all steamboat wrecks were caused by submerged trees. The nineteenth-century western missionary Father Pierre Jean De Smet summed up steamboat travel for many wary passengers:

> I will only remind you that steam navigation on the Missouri is one of the most dangerous things a man can undertake. I fear the sea, but all the storms and other unpleasant things I have experienced in four different ocean voyages did not inspire me with so much terror as the navigation of the somber, treacherous, muddy Missouri.[54]

From 1838 until the 1880s, the U.S. government undertook the herculean effort of clearing the Missouri of all river obstructions, including trees and snags. The U.S. Army Corps of Engineers was engaged in the task, and, in 1838, two government snagboats, the *Heliopolis* and *Archimedes,* began their work on the Lower Missouri. It was a massive effort. On the lower 300 miles of the river, the two boat crews "removed 2,245 snags and cut 1,710 overhanging trees that appeared on the verge of dropping into the river."[55] Snags were removed with the aid of a machine-operated pulley system that included steel cables and chains. The project proved so extensive that it was impossible for the government to complete the work. During just one 13-year period, the Army Corps of Engineers removed nearly 18,000 snags from the muddy Missouri, most from the lower river because most of the riverboat traffic was concentrated in those waters.

Much of the effort to remove snags was halted after 1880. The railroads had arrived on the banks of the Missouri during the preceding 20 years, including in the river towns of St. Joseph, Missouri (1859); Council Bluffs and Sioux City, Iowa (1867 and 1868, respectively); and Pierre and Chamberlain, in the Dakota Territory (1880 and 1881, respectively). With the arrival of the railroads, the steamboat that continued on the river ran shorter distances from one rail–river town to the next. The Great Northern Railroad even reached Helena, in the Montana Territory, by 1887, ending long-distance steamboat navigation on the Missouri.

As the steamboat era on the Missouri slipped onto the pages of history, the Missouri River entered a desultory period. Few boats plied the Upper Missouri, and most of them delivered supplies from Bismarck to Fort Benton. However, the river was not completely abandoned. During the 1880s and 1890s, several river communities joined in an effort to change the river from one dependent on steamboat navigation to a barge waterway. The leading citizens of Sioux City, Omaha, St. Joseph, Leavenworth, and Kansas City began petitioning the federal government to "channelize the Missouri to inaugurate deep-draft barge traffic."[56] The people of these important river trade communities believed that only barges could compete with the ever-encroaching tentacles of the western railroads. Another impetus for channelization on the Missouri was the disastrous flood of 1881.

The Flood of 1881 technically began as a snowstorm in 1880.

HARDLY A LARGE BARGE

Although barge traffic on such inland rivers as the Mississippi and Ohio became big business by the 1930s and 1940s, barging on the Missouri River never caught on. Despite the extensive channeling of the river's course, barge traffic was always limited and elusive, a disappointment to the businessmen in several key Missouri River towns and cities, including Kansas City, Omaha, and Sioux City.

By the 1940s, many had come to believe that the opening of Fort Peck Dam would lead to greater barge traffic on the river. In Sioux City, an attempt to establish barge service on the river failed miserably. During the fall of 1940, a group of businessmen formed the Sioux City–New Orleans Barge Line. Its name implied the company's intention: to begin shipping barge freight downriver from Iowa all the way to the Mississippi River port of New Orleans.

Everything quickly went wrong. The company's first towboat, the *Sioux City,* was underpowered, boasting a 110-horsepower engine, "barely enough power to push one deep-draft barge designed for service on the Mississippi."* To add to the company's errors, the *Sioux City* was designed so poorly that the captain of the towboat, standing in the pilothouse, could not see the river from the stern of the barge. A crewman was forced to take a position at the head of the barge and cautiously shout information to the pilothouse so the pilot would know when and where to turn the barge on the river.

In addition, the *Sioux City* made its maiden voyage with only 200 tons of cargo, approximately one-quarter of its design capacity. The barge was so lightly loaded because the river was low and, if fully loaded, the barge would have "struck bottom so frequently that it might never have reached its final destination."**

  * Quoted in Schneiders, Unruly River, 146.

** Ibid.

As early as October that year, heavy winter storms struck across the Great Plains and the Missouri River Valley. Temperatures plummeted, freezing the river by November. The following months caused the surface ice on the Missouri to reach a thickness of four feet. Heavy snows piled onto the frozen waters of the river and across the Dakota and Montana landscapes, creating a snow pack of at least four feet. Then, in March 1881, warm southern winds began to thaw out the Dakotas and Montana, sending six months of water down the quickly inundated Missouri's path. The results were disastrous:

> Once unleashed, the Missouri plowed downstream, bulldozing the ice sheet in front of it, pulling up blocks of ice like shingles from a roof and then throwing the fragments to the sides. The river literally rumbled as it descended the valley, gaining momentum below Bismarck when sudden warm temperatures and rain dissolved the heavy snow cover, feeding water into the swelling stream. The high water, ice, and flotsam formed a particularly destructive mixture.[57]

The flood wiped out whole towns along the river as the waters of the Missouri crested 41 feet above normal level. Some towns were completely abandoned by the river as the furious Missouri rerouted its course across flooded lowlands. The Dakota towns of Yankton, Green Island, Vermillion, Burbank, and Elk Point were among some of the hardest hit. After the floodwaters subsided, Green Island had only one building still standing on its foundations.

The 1881 flood only increased the call for the channelization and dredging of the Missouri River. Congress finally passed the Act for the General Improvement of the Missouri River in 1882, earmarking $850,000 for the project. In addition, Congress ordered the Corps of Engineers to step up its snag removal program and to restabilize the banks of the river that had been destroyed by the monstrous flood. The channelization project fell into the hands of Major Charles Suter, who gathered a river flotilla of nearly 200 boats, "including mattress boats, barges, snagboats, hydraulic graders, hydraulic pile drivers, quarter-boats, yawls, skiffs, and a floating machine shop."[58] In fact, Suter spent nearly all the money allotted by Congress just raising his fleet of river craft. Congress, committed to the channelization project, soon allocated additional funds.

Though the Missouri River was a valuable route for trade and migration in the nineteenth century, it was also a dangerous means of transportation. The river's swift currents combined with obstructions such as submerged trees, as seen in this painting of a Punka Indian encampment, made travel on the river extremely treacherous.

Over the next decade, millions of dollars were earmarked for the channelization of the river. Major Suter pushed his project along. As he examined the river during the early days of the project, Suter had determined that the Missouri was a large enough river to maintain a 12-foot channel from Sioux City, Iowa, to its mouth, even during years of low-flow. By the early 1890s, however, the project was regeared to create an eight-foot-deep channel with a width of 850 feet. Channelization itself—the routing of the river—was established by the Corps' construction of artificial banks made of long white oak and cypress poles driven into the river bed. These poles—often called piles—typically measured between 30 and 50 feet in length with a diameter similar to a telephone pole. The piles were driven into the riverbanks with hydraulic pile drivers, the early models powered by steam and later models fueled by diesel oil. Approximately 600 or 700 blows from the pile driver were required to drive the piles to an adequate depth. Then the piles were connected by pine boards and covered over with willow saplings, forming a "willow curtain, which served the purpose of further slowing the river's current. As the current slowed on the downstream side of the willow curtain, the water no longer had the momentum to carry its silt load, so it dropped the silt on the downstream side of the pile dike." [59]

The channelization project made slow progress through the 1890s. Only another natural disaster on the Missouri River— the Flood of 1903—revived the river channelization program. Although the flood that year was limited to the Kansas City region and regions downriver, it proved to be as costly a flood as any that had hit the Missouri system to that date. The flood inundated two-thirds of a million acres of farmland, and property damage in the two Kansas Cities (Missouri and Kansas) totaled more than $1 million. After additional floods hit the river the following two years, new voices were raised in favor of developing a flood-control program. In 1906, in an effort to prove the viability of barge navigation on the Missouri, a group of Missouri businessmen chartered a pair of steamboats to push two barges loaded with freight up the river from St. Louis to Kansas City. Although Congress appeared uninterested in funding additional rechannelization, President Theodore Roosevelt did push for the project, having become convinced that America's inland waterways needed to be revitalized and tapped for twentieth-century commerce. To the progressive Roosevelt, "failure to develop the rivers of the United States constituted the waste of a valuable resource." [60] With President Roosevelt's support, plus the added incentive of

The flood of 1903 devastated the Kansas City region and areas south along the Missouri. The debris shown in this photograph is just a small part of the one million dollars in property damage caused by the flooding. Frequent flooding along the river prompted the government to initiate channelization projects to better control the Missouri.

another devastating flood on the Missouri in 1908, rechannelization received renewed promotion.

With more federal money being authorized annually, the Missouri River channelization project gained new critics. Those opposed to the expensive project repeated claims made in earlier decades, insisting that "Missouri River barge traffic would never reach levels necessary to justify the expense of constructing the navigation channel."[61] One member of the Board of Engineers of the Corps of Engineers even suggested that all channeling be halted and federal funding for the river be limited to $40,000 annually for the removal of snags. World War I did cause a reduction in federal funding on nearly all American inland waterway projects, including the work being done on the Missouri River, and, by 1916, progress on the Missouri River navigation channel ground to a halt. Even after the war, channelization did not resume. Between 1916 and 1922, the Army Corps of Engineers spent just $1 million, not even enough money to maintain the already existing channelization systems. As late as 1922, only one of every three miles of the Lower Missouri between St. Charles and Kansas City had been channeled. Upriver, above Kansas City, no channeling had even taken place. Not surprisingly, nearly all deep-draft steamboats and barges stayed off the Missouri, plying the waters of the deeper Mississippi River instead. Almost $7.5 million had been spent in channeling just 135 miles of the Lower Missouri.

For the next five years, little improvement came to the Missouri River in the form of channeling or river maintenance in general. Yet Missouri River businessmen, farmers, and other river commercial interests continued to lobby Congress for additional channeling support. Then, in 1927, Congress passed the Upper River Project, designed to improve river navigation on the river between Kansas City, Missouri and Sioux City, Iowa. Funding on the Lower Missouri was also approved, and the channel depth was altered to nine feet, the same depth to which the Mississippi River was being channeled at that time. Missouri interests knew that barge traffic would never develop on the Missouri if Mississippi barges could not move up the Missouri River.

Over the next 15 years, the changes introduced on the Missouri River were significant:

> By 1932 the Corps had confined the river below Kansas City into a single channel. From 1932 to 1940 it channelized most of the 385 miles of river between Kansas City and Sioux City. At the same time that the channelization project progressed

along the lower river, federal engineers built Fort Peck Dam. In summer 1937 the Corps closed the massive dam and its reservoir began to fill with water, eventually creating a man-made lake 134 miles long. By the end of 1942, 750 miles of the lower river and 134 miles of the upper river barely resembled the Missouri's former character.[62]

The changes were extensive, and they did not occur overnight. The scale of improvements made on the Missouri River during those years was like nothing seen in the river's history. One significant incentive in the intensity and scope of developing the Missouri River Valley was simple economics. By 1929, the United States was slipping into a national depression, a significant downturn in the economy, which led to 25 percent unemployment. The government became intent on creating job programs for the unemployed, which led to the hiring of thousands of workers on Missouri River improvement programs. Between 1929 and 1932, the Army Corps of Engineers, and the private firms with which it contracted, hired as many as 13,000 river workers for improvements then underway on the Lower Missouri alone. These men worked on pile-driving boats and on other channeling projects. Although the work was largely seasonal, with almost no one working the river during the winter months, with each spring thousands were reemployed. Most of the workers on the Missouri River projects were locals, men who lived in river towns or on farms in close proximity to the river. They did their jobs largely as unskilled laborers, carrying out the difficult, often backbreaking labor of cutting and hauling stone or working along the river banks, cutting willows and weaving the willow branch "mattresses" that were designed to protect the river's banks or create new embankments.

Then, in 1932, President Franklin Roosevelt was elected, and his commitment to such river projects as those on the Missouri River was significant. Still, the thrust of improvements on the Missouri was about to undergo significant alteration. The

Army Corps of Engineers had spent nearly half a century focusing on rechanneling the river, but a drought on the Great Plains was forcing many to look at the Missouri River in a different light. All previous channeling efforts had assumed that the Missouri's water flow would never drop so low that barge traffic would not even be possible. However, the Dust Bowl era of the 1930s caused drastic changes in the river's depth. From 1929 through 1931, "the river below Sioux City did not meet [the] minimum-depth requirement [for barge traffic] for a total of 413 days, more than half the barge navigation season."[63] For more than two months in 1931, the river below Kansas City failed to contain enough water for barges. Suddenly, all assumptions concerning the river's water flow and its capacity to maintain a consistent channel for barge traffic vanished. For the Army Corps of Engineers, this new reality caused a significant turn in thought about the Missouri River. The Corps quickly called for "the construction of upstream storage reservoirs either on the Missouri main stem or one of its larger tributaries."[64] Such dams could be used to control the water flow of the Missouri, creating vast reservoirs of water that could be released periodically to increase the water flow on the river during periods of low water level. Before the Corps was finished, it would oversee the construction of six major dams on the Missouri River, from South Dakota to Montana, during the following 30 years. These dams would change the western waterway dramatically and create yet another era in the history of the Missouri River Valley.

The building of the Fort Peck Dam, the first of the Missouri River reservoir projects, constituted an extensive construction project. During the early 1930s, the Army Corps of Engineers examined possible sites for a dam and, by 1932, had narrowed the possibilities down to two. The Corps considered building a dam on the Kaw River, a Missouri tributary near Topeka, Kansas, west of Kansas City. Otherwise, they looked to the Upper Missouri at Fort Peck in Montana. In time, the Corps selected the Fort Peck site.

Within 100 days of President Franklin Roosevelt taking office as the 32nd president of the United States, Congress passed legislation creating a New Deal agency, the Public Works Administration, which was allocated a budget of $3.3 billion. Just days after the legislation was passed, the Army Corps of Engineers held hearings in Washington concerning river improvements on the Missouri. Within two weeks, the War Department submitted a request from the PWA for $17 million to kick-start Missouri River channelization. By mid-August, the funding was approved by PWA chief Harold Ickes. Of the $17 million authorized, more than $14 million was earmarked for the Upper Missouri. Channelization had struggled to make progress for decades, and once again, basic economics restarted the project. The Missouri Valley region was home to tens of thousands of unemployed workers. In Sioux City alone, one out of every five citizens was in a welfare program. The PWA program would provide a much-needed shot in the arm for the people of the region. In October 1933, in the wake of this revitalizing of the channeling of the Missouri, the Roosevelt administration authorized $15.5 million for the construction of the Fort Peck Dam.

Events immediately swung into high gear. Just days after the allotment of PWA funds for the Fort Peck Dam, the district engineer, Theodore Wyman, hired 70 men to begin clearing underbrush and timber from the proposed dam site. Then, in January 1934, construction of several dredge boats, designed to "suck clay from the riverbed and deposit the material on the dam embankment" was underway.[65] The next month, 1,000 workers were on the dam site, the majority from Valley County, Montana, just north of the Missouri River.

As the construction on the dam developed, the full scope of the project became evident. It was more than just building a dam. There were electrical lines to be laid, a railroad-bridge was constructed downriver, 28-foot-diameter tunnels were cut to divert the Missouri River from its natural bed, and the movement of earth and stone seemed limitless. Much of the work

The election of President Franklin D. Roosevelt in 1932 meant big changes to the Missouri and its surrounding areas. One of Roosevelt's New Deal agencies, the Public Works Administration, went to work in the Missouri Valley, restructuring the river while providing jobs for many of the thousands of unemployed valley residents. The Roosevelt administration oversaw the rechanneling of the river, in addition to the removal of trees and snags, and the construction of several dams.

at the dam site for the first year involved these infrastructure necessities rather than the dam itself. The original funding for the project was augmented when Harold Ickes funneled another $25 million of PWA money by the summer of 1934. In August, President Roosevelt visited the Fort Peck site to observe the progress. While looking "down on the dusty, windswept dam site from the hills above, the president proudly observed 7,000 bronzed men erecting an edifice in his name." [66]

Meanwhile, work was underway on the Upper River Project to rechannel the Missouri. Thousands were at work on the river's course between St. Joseph, Missouri, and Sioux City, Iowa. With plenty of federal money available and an endless supply of workers, much of the six-foot channel of the Missouri between those two cities was finished by the summer of 1934. Channeling on the river continued through the 1930s, receiving repeated funding from either the PWA or the Works Progress Administration (WPA). As the Missouri River underwent an extensive restructuring, a twentieth-century taming, snagboats on the river remained extremely busy. From 1936 to 1937, the Army Corps of Engineers removed nearly 800 snags from the river. An additional 9,000 trees, considered threats to the river, were cut from the river's banks just between Kansas City and Sioux City. During just the decade of the 1930s, more river trees were cut down by the Army Corps than had been removed during the era of the Missouri River steamboats.

Back upriver, the backbreaking work of constructing the Fort Peck Dam continued through the late 1930s. At the height of construction, 10,000 people were at work on the dam. Although water was diverted into the four massive flood control tunnels during the summer of 1937, three more years passed before the project was completed. As Fort Peck Dam began containing the waters of the Missouri River, a lake formed behind the dam, measuring 180 miles in length and 16 miles across at its widest point. This huge Fort Peck Reservoir held enough water "to cover the entire state of Montana 2½ inches deep.[67] Yet even as the Fort Peck Dam project was completed and the channelization project completed to Sioux City, Iowa, the Missouri River saw little barge traffic as a result.

7

The Modern Missouri

With the opening of the Fort Peck Dam, the future of the Missouri River took a serious turn. The dam retained millions of gallons of water and was designed to help alleviate the threat of flooding on the Missouri and to regulate the water level of the increasingly channeled river. In the spring of 1943, floods once again inundated the bottomlands of North and South Dakota, downriver from the Fort Peck facility. Much of the flooding was centered between Yankton, South Dakota, and Omaha, Nebraska, as "two of the Missouri's largest tributaries, the James and the Big Sioux, dumped fantastic amounts of water into the already swollen river."[68] At Yankton, the flooded Missouri nearly exceeded its 1881 flood stage. Residents of towns along the Middle Missouri found themselves living in a vast silt-laden sea as the Missouri overflowed its banks. In Sioux City, police commandeered dozens of johnboats (narrow flat-bottomed boats) to aid in the rescue of those stranded by the floodwaters. As floods struck even farther downriver, they filled up the channeled portion of the Missouri near Kansas City, spilling out over more than a half-million acres of prime Missouri farmland.

Given the scope of the 1943 spring floods, new calls soon arose for additional dam construction to further control the excesses of the river. In late May, the governors of Iowa, Missouri, and Kansas joined with the Upper Missouri River states of Nebraska, the Dakotas, and Montana to discuss their flood problems and future dam projects. These state leaders determined that nearly all future dams designed to seriously limit flooding on the Missouri would need to be built in South Dakota. Several geographical and economic factors played a role in that decision. Building dams south of Yankton would not be cost-effective, and any dams and reservoirs built in North Dakota and Montana "would not capture enough tributary runoff to significantly lower flood levels at Omaha, St. Joseph, and Kansas City."[69]

Even before the floods of the spring of 1943 had subsided completely, residents along the river appealed to the federal government and the U.S. Army Corps of Engineers to authorize

Severe flooding in 1943 proved that additional dams were needed along the Missouri in South Dakota to prevent flooding further downriver. One such dam project authorized at this time was the Garrison Dam near Bismarck, North Dakota, shown here.

additional dam projects. Much of the responsibility for these dams fell to Colonel Lewis Pick, then head of the Missouri River Division, which included the Missouri River Valley from Fort Peck to Kansas City. After studying the river during the summer of 1943, Pick was convinced that a series of dams on the Missouri should come under construction as soon as World War II ended. In a speech in Sioux City, he stated, "The Missouri River Valley is the last great valley in the United States whose water potentialities have not been developed. . . . If the river is not properly under control the results will be disastrous."[70] Once a new and extensive dam system was built, assured Pick, it would provide "a source of power to pump water for irrigation, keep the proposed [nine-foot] navigation channel open even in low water seasons and operate industrial and electrical plants."[71]

Pick submitted his plans to Congress that fall, calling for the construction of four immense earthen-fill dams in both North and South Dakota. These dams would be constructed in places along the river far enough upstream to catch much of the spring runoff while maintaining the nine-foot navigation channel south of Sioux City (even though the nine-foot channel had yet to be completed). Pick's plan called for dams to be built at Garrison, North Dakota, as well as at three South Dakota sites, including Oahe (near Pierre, the state capital), Fort Randall (Lake Andes), and Gavin's Point (outside Yankton). In addition, Colonel Pick's blueprints proposed the building of "low, re-regulating dams below the bigger dams, which would eliminate destructive water surges when the big dams released large amounts of water."[72] These secondary dams would help limit riverbank erosion and the disruption of downriver navigation.

In late 1943, the Army Corps presented its plan to Congress. Over the intervening months, controversy developed between the Corps and the Bureau of Reclamation, which submitted its own plan for building dams. The challenge proposal, called the Sloan Plan after a Montana Bureau of Management field agent, recognized the necessity of building dams in South Dakota but omitted the Garrison Dam and the Gavin's Point facility. An eventual compromise led to the Pick–Sloan Plan, which called for the building of five dams in North Dakota and South Dakota. The Oahe, Big Bend, Fort Randall, and Gavin's Point facilities would be constructed in South Dakota, and the Garrison Dam was slated for North Dakota. One of the facilities, the Big Bend Dam, was to be built at a slightly different site than the Corps of Engineers had earlier suggested. In December 1944, President Roosevelt signed the congressional legislation authorizing the construction of the five dams agreed upon under the Pick–Sloan Plan. The following spring, Congress also authorized the construction of the nine-foot navigation channel from St. Charles, Missouri, to Sioux City, Iowa.

When World War II ended in 1945, construction was organized on two of the multidam projects: Fort Randall and Garrison. The Fort Randall facility was considered the centerpiece of the entire multidam system, given its "location far down along the Missouri main stem."[73] Engineers for the Army Corps believed that the Fort Randall Dam would help reduce any Missouri flood crest by four feet, a significant level. By the fall of 1946, dam building was underway.

Because the Fort Randall Dam was an earth-fill structure, much of the work was the transportation of massive amounts of rock and earth. Work on the embankment did not begin until 1948, but by the spring of 1952, the completed portion of the dam towered 185 feet in height and extended across the Missouri a distance of 8,000 feet, more than a mile and a half. At its base, the dam measured 1,600 feet wide. This section of the dam alone required the dumping of 30 million cubic yards of dirt, and there remained another length of 1,000 feet to complete the dam. Then, just as the lion's share of the construction of Fort Randall Dam had been finished, nature threw yet another curve at the Missouri River.

High snowfall across the Dakotas and Montana caused some experts to predict a flood on the river that spring. By April 1, the snows stretching across the northern Great Plains and the eastern Rockies had begun to melt, producing massive quantities of water. Soon, most of the upriver tributaries of the Missouri were filled to capacity, becoming "raging torrents, spilling out across their valleys, hurling debris down their channels, and racing toward the main stem of the Missouri."[74] Floods soon rampaged across North Dakota, hitting Bismarck hard, inundating the town's rail tracks and destroying homes along the river's banks. A week later, much of Pierre, South Dakota, was underwater. At Chamberlain, South Dakota, a section of the Milwaukee Railroad Bridge, which spanned the Missouri, gave way and fell into the river.

Sioux City received the worst of the violent flood. On Easter Sunday, April 13, the city was completely evacuated, and flood-waters covered nearly every neighborhood. The town's business district was destroyed, and the city's stockyards became a swampy morass of silty water, ice chunks, and cattle waste. The devastating natural disaster caused nearly $50 million in property damage, including "washing out roads, undermining bridges, and carrying away long sections of railroad."[75] Farther downriver, the city of Omaha braced for the flood's impact, placing its hope in a levee system that had been constructed after the 1943 flood. At Omaha and Council Bluffs across the river, the Corps of Engineers had built a 1,200-foot-wide channel flanked by 12 miles of levee. The man-made embankment— designed to withstand a river crest of 31½ feet—was reinforced with an additional three feet of sandbags. As the floodwaters crested on the night of April 17, the residents of the two Missouri River cities watched anxiously as the river crested at 30 feet, leaving the levee intact and Omaha–Council Bluffs safe from the harsh realities of flooding. Downriver, however, residents of the state of Missouri experienced flooding that produced more than $50 million in property damage. Miraculously, the entire Missouri River Valley flood caused no human deaths.

In the aftermath of this devastating flood, the construction of the Missouri River dam system received even greater support. Congress had cut funding for the Gavin's Point Dam and the Oahe Dam, but the flood engendered so much public outrage that both projects received significant appropriations to begin construction. In addition, by November 1952, work on the Fort Randall Dam was largely completed and the dam's reservoir began to fill. Throughout the summer, the man-made lake stretched from the dam to a distance of 23 miles. That fall, the Fort Randall reservoir covered 45,000 square acres. After two years, the lake reached Chamberlain, South Dakota, 90 miles upstream from the dam.

With the opening of Fort Randall Dam, the process of channeling the river south of Sioux City moved ahead, because the dam cut down on the Missouri River's capacity to erode its embankments and rechannel itself. Through the 1950s and 1960s, the channelization process reached its farthest extensions, until, by 1970, the channel from Sioux City to the river's mouth was finally completed. By 1955, the Gavin's Point Dam was closed, followed by the Oahe Dam in 1958 and the Big Bend Dam five years later. Of the dams constructed on the Missouri River, they fall into two categories—large storage facilities and control dams. The storage dams, including Fort Peck, Garrison, and Oahe, are those farthest upstream on the river. Each of the three is capable of storing 25 million acre-feet of water. Together, they can contain enough water to equal three years of the Missouri River's annual flow. However, the amounts they store are considerably less, with Fort Peck holding approximately a quarter-million acre-feet; Garrison, 368,000 acre-feet; and Oahe, 371,000 acre-feet. The control dams impound less: Big Bend holds 61,000 acre-feet; Fort Randall, 102,000 acre-feet; and the smallest, Gavin's Point, holds 32,000 acre-feet. In addition to the Fort Peck Dam in Montana, nine dams have been built in that state, including facilities such as Toston, Canyon Ferry, Hauser, Holter, Black Eagle, Morony, Ryan, Cochrane, and Great Falls.

The building of the extensive dam system on the Missouri changed the river in many ways, and the closing of these massive earthen obstacles "set off a series of physical and ecological changes in the river corridor, which occurred both simultaneously and over a short period of time."[76] With the Army Corps of Engineers holding the power of the Missouri River within established river corridors, the natural system of flood plains began to dry up. With the dams producing a manipulated flow of water, this "markedly decreased the river's ability to erode, meander, and flood."[77] This single alteration of the river's natural ebb and flow caused a serious reduction in and wholesale destruction of the wetlands and breeding grounds of a wide variety of water birds that migrated along the river's corridor.

The dam system and its gigantic holding reservoirs also significantly reduced the amount of silt in the water. Before the

Despite the government's attempt to corral the river, the Missouri continued to flood throughout the twentieth century. The flood of 1993 was so severe that it destroyed many man-made channel dikes and barriers and returned to its natural flow in some areas. This small jet at the Spirit of St. Louis airport in Missouri was one casualty when the river overflowed its banks in 1993.

opening of the South Dakota dams, the Missouri probably carried 142 million tons of silt past Sioux City annually. After the dams came on line, the silt content was reduced to 4 million tons. For many living along the Missouri's banks, the old nickname for the river—Big Muddy—no longer rang true. The changes in the river brought on by modern technology and a general retooling by the Army Corps of Engineers caused the river to erode its bed to a greater extent, causing the bed to lower, a problem that continued into the 1980s. As the river naturally deepened itself, the Missouri experienced the arrival of a new type of rivercraft: V-bottomed sport boats powered by giant engines, some as large as 500-horsepower.

Along the river, a new economic center developed with "a supporting system of harbors, gas stations, convenience stores, and restaurants."[78]

Throughout the 1980s and 1990s, the river witnessed a dramatic increase in sports boating, and it also experienced serious changes in its fish population and diversity. In the 1980s, the river was dominated by three types of fish: carp, buffalo fish, and channel catfish. Others, including shovelnose sturgeon, flathead catfish, paddlefish, gar, and pike, were dropping in numbers, and fish hatcheries worked feverishly to maintain any paddlefish on the river. However, the clearer waters of the Missouri also gave rise to fish types that could never have survived in the silt-thick waters of the earlier river, including trout and salmon.

As for flooding on the river in the final decades of the twentieth century, the system of dams did not bring such stark realities to an end. Floods occurred along the main corridor of the Missouri in 1960, 1971, 1973, 1984, 1993, and 1995. At the same time, the channeling of the river, a project that had taken most of a century, never translated into significant barge traffic. Even as late as 1979, the Missouri River carried less than 1 percent of the nation's barge tonnage. (That year the Missouri carried 2.4 million tons and the Mississippi River floated 300 million tons!)

The 1990s did bring some restoration of the natural systems of the river. Following suggestions voiced by such environmental groups as the Audubon Society and American Rivers, programs were established to reopen "former channel areas within the river corridor since allowing water to flow through the natural channel would benefit both people and wildlife."[79] Nature lent its own hand in this effort with the Flood of 1993. That year, Missouri River flooding destroyed miles of channel dikes, which allowed the river to refill former channel areas, cut new channels, and reinstate habitat lands. As the Army Corps of Engineers moved quickly to rebuild its lost barriers to the river's channel, environmentalists called for the re-created river to return to some of its wilder origins.

THE WILDER SIDE OF THE MISSOURI RIVER

Efforts were undertaken during the twentieth century to tame the Lower Missouri River, but on the Upper Missouri, significant efforts were made to leave the river and its surrounding lands in a state of union with nature.

In an effort to preserve the natural state of the Missouri region while setting aside land for wildlife, the Charles M. Russell National Wildlife Refuge (CMR) was established in 1936. The refuge follows 220 miles of the Missouri River and includes tens of thousands of acres of pristine, unspoiled natural beauty, most notably the rugged hills of the Missouri River Breaks. In the midst of the CMR lies Fort Peck Lake.

CMR is the second-largest national wildlife refuge in the lower 48 states. Today, the CMR is home to an abundance of Missouri River wildlife, including 40 species of mammals, including white-tailed deer, mule deer, and antelope. Four thousand acres of prairie dog villages dot the refuge lands. The CMR is also home to 200 species of birds, 17 types of fish—including large paddle-fish, which are highly prized by fishermen—and more than a dozen species of amphibians and reptiles.

Through much of this virgin country, the Missouri River follows an old course, having changed channels little over the centuries. At a portion of the refuge known as UL Bend Wilderness, the river twists and turns through the region so extensively that nineteenth-century steamboat passengers "would disembark and hike a short distance across—perhaps a mile or two—and wait for the boat to make the 10 to12-mile journey around the U-shaped river bend."[*]

Whether viewed through the eyes of an early Native American, a nineteenth-century steamboat passenger, or a modern-day hiker, the CMR remains a "magnificent river segment . . . rich beyond measure in scenic, recreational, wildlife, historical, archeological, and geological values. . . . It is priceless to the nation."[**]

[*] Quoted in Gildart, *Montana's Missouri River,* 71.

[**] Ibid., 100.

In the decade after the Flood of 1993, the Missouri remained a river of hopes and dreams, plans and schemes, nature versus the Army Corps of Engineers. What the future holds for the river remains the great looming question from Montana downstream

Despite all the alterations to the river, it remains a force of beauty and power. In this photograph the Missouri is seen through the "Eye of the Needle," a natural arch on the cliffs above the river in central Montana.

to Missouri, thousands of miles away. Various groups battle over the direction of the river, each intent on pursuing its own goals for the river and how it may serve their interests. As historian Robert Schneiders writes,

> By 1995, the Missouri River flowed through a land of discontent. Few people expressed satisfaction with the engineered river and its government overseers. This general discord and uneasiness stemmed from one simple, irrefutable truth; the Missouri compelled people to look at themselves and to question their faith in technology, their commitment to progress, and their motives.[80]

The modern Missouri River continues to flow from its western Montana headwaters to the Mississippi, providing for the people who share its banks a quality of life greater than that of any generation that has ever lived within its meandering valleys and channelized courses. Although the twenty-first-century Missouri holds fewer mysteries than it held in the past, it remains a river of beauty, power, challenge, and change. To stand on its banks and watch it roll beside its mountain straits, sandstone rock formations, prairie meadows, meandering bottomlands, and even its towns and metropolitan centers is to be reminded of the words written by the nineteenth-century American poet Walt Whitman:

> Others may praise what they like;
>
> But I, from the banks of the running Missouri,
>   Praise nothing, in art, or aught else,
>
> 'Till it has breathed well the atmosphere of this
>   river—also the western prairie-scent,
>
> And fully exudes it again.[81]

10,000 B.C. Anthropologists date many of the first Indian arrivals to the Missouri River region and the Great Plains to this time.

7000–4500 B.C. Many of the human inhabitants of the Great Plains abandon the region due to a prolonged drought.

500 B.C.–A.D. 1000 A fairly advanced village existence develops along the Missouri River Valley.

A.D. 800 Important Native American tribes have settled along the Missouri River.

A.D. 1500 Modern tribal systems have been established for those Indians living along the Missouri River.

1673 Father Jacques Marquette, French explorer, arrives at the mouth of the Missouri River while traveling down the Mississippi River.

500 B.C.–A.D. 1000
A fairly advanced village existence has developed along the Missouri River Valley.

1783
Frenchman, Sieur de La Verendrye, reaches the Upper Missouri from Canada.

1714
First European, Frenchman Etienne Venyard de Bourgmont makes voyage up the Missouri River.

500 B.C.–A.D. 1000 ———— 1700 ———— 1820

1673
Father Jacques Marquette, French explorer, arrives at the mouth of the Missouri River.

1804–06
Explorers Meriwether Lewis and William Clark lead the Corps of Discovery up the Missouri River.

1819
The first steamboat, the Independence, reaches the Missouri River.

1600s–1700s French fur trappers actively trade with Missouri River Indians.

1700s Horses arrive on the North Great Plains, allowing Missouri River tribes to engage in extensive horse and buffalo culture.

1714 Frenchman Etienne Venyard de Bourgmont makes a voyage up the Missouri River and becomes the first European to explore, chart, and describe the river.

1783 Pierre Gaultier de Varennes, Sieur de La Verendrye, a Frenchman, arrives on the banks of the Upper Missouri after reaching the region from Canada.

1803 French sell the Louisiana Territory to the United States, making the Missouri River Valley American territory.

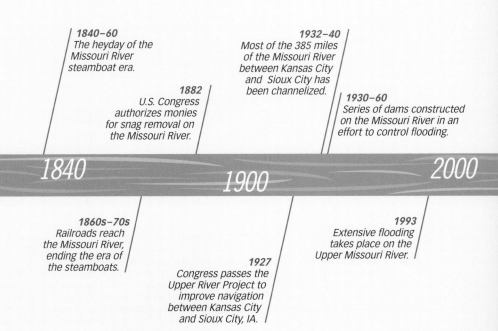

1840–60
The heyday of the Missouri River steamboat era.

1882
U.S. Congress authorizes monies for snag removal on the Missouri River.

1932–40
Most of the 385 miles of the Missouri River between Kansas City and Sioux City has been channelized.

1930–60
Series of dams constructed on the Missouri River in an effort to control flooding.

1840 **1900** **2000**

1860s–70s
Railroads reach the Missouri River, ending the era of the steamboats.

1927
Congress passes the Upper River Project to improve navigation between Kansas City and Sioux City, IA.

1993
Extensive flooding takes place on the Upper Missouri River.

1804–6 American explorers Meriwether Lewis and
William Clark lead the Corps of Discovery up
the Missouri River.

1806 Fur entrepreneur Manuel Lisa establishes his Upper
Missouri trading company, the Missouri Fur Company.

1819 The first steamboat, the *Independence,* reaches the
Missouri River That year, the steamboat *Western
Engineer* reaches the confluence of the Kansas and
Missouri Rivers.

1828 Kenneth McKenzie opens his Upper Missouri Outfit
on the Missouri River and expands the fur trade.

1830s American artist George Catlin produces hundreds of
paintings and watercolors of the Native American
life on the Missouri River.

1830 Fort Union, on the Upper Missouri, is opened for
the fur trade business.

1833 German naturalist Prince Maximilian and Swiss
artist Karl Bodmer document the cultural and
natural history of the Upper Missouri River.

1837 The Missouri River witnesses an extensive and
deadly outbreak of smallpox, which kills thousands
of Great Plains Indians.

1840–60 The heyday of the Missouri River steamboat era
lasts for two decades.

1859 Approximately 100 steamboats ply the waters of
the Missouri River.

1860s–70s Railroads reach the Missouri River, ending the era
of the Missouri River steamboats.

1881 Extensive flooding on the Missouri River.

1882 U.S. Congress authorizes monies for snag removal on the Missouri River.

1903 Another damaging flood on the Missouri, which spurs the river channelization program.

1927 Congress passes the Upper River Project, designed to improve river navigation between Kansas City, Missouri, and Sioux City, Iowa.

1932 By this year, the U.S. Army Corps of Engineers has confined the Missouri River below Kansas City to a single channel.

1932–40 Most of the 385 miles of the Missouri River have been channelized between Kansas City and Sioux City.

1937 Work on the Fort Peck Dam is completed.

1943 Missouri River experiences another severe flood, leading to the development of an extensive dam system on the river.

1944 President Franklin Roosevelt signs the congressional legislation for the Pick–Sloan Plan, which determines the dam projects that will be built on the river through the 1950s.

1952 Work on the Fort Randall Dam is largely completed and the dam's reservoir begins to fill.

1955 Gavin's Point Dam is completed.

1958 Oahe Dam is completed.

1980s–90s Development of extensive sports fishing on the Missouri River.

1993 Extensive flooding takes place on the Upper Missouri River.

NOTES

CHAPTER 1

1. Quoted in Daniel B. Botkin, *Passage of Discovery: The American Rivers Guide to the Missouri River of Lewis and Clark* (New York: Perigee Books, 1999), 77.

2. Quoted in Stanley Vestal, *The Missouri* (Lincoln: University of Nebraska Press, 1945), 15.

3. Quoted in Robert Kelley Schneiders, *Unruly River: Two Centuries of Change Along the Missouri* (Lawrence: University Press of Kansas, 1999), 12.

4. Quoted in Vestal, *The Missouri*, 12.

5. Quoted in Alvin M. Josephy, Jr. *The Indian Heritage of America* (Boston: Houghton Mifflin, 1991), 113.

6. Quoted in "The Cellars of Time: Paleontology and Archaeology in Nebraska," *Nebraska History*, 75, no. 1 (1994): 136.

7. Quoted in Vestal, *The Missouri*, 14.

CHAPTER 2

8. Quoted in Michael Gillespie, *Wild River, Wooden Boats: True Stories of Steamboating and the Missouri River* (Stoddard, WI: Heritage Press, 2000), 3.

9. Quoted in W. Raymond Wood, *Prologue to Lewis and Clark: The Mackay and Evans Expedition* (Norman: University of Oklahoma Press, 2003), 13.

10. Quoted in Vestal, *The Missouri*, 61.

11. Ibid.

12. Quoted in Tanis C. Thorne, *The Many Hands of My Relations: French and Indians on the Lower Missouri* (Columbia: University of Missouri Press, 1996), 59.

13. Ibid.

14. Quoted in Vestal, *The Missouri*, 64.

15. Ibid.

16. Ibid., 68.

17. Quoted in Stephen Ambrose, *Undaunted Courage: Meriwether Lewis, Thomas Jefferson, and the Opening of the American West* (New York: Simon & Schuster, 1996), 104.

CHAPTER 3

18. Quoted in Bernard DeVoto, *The Journals of Lewis and Clark* (Boston: Houghton Mifflin, 1981), 9.

19. Quoted in Barbara Fifer and Vicky Soderberg, *Along the Trail With Lewis and Clark* (Helena: Montana Magazine, Inc., 2001), 50.

20. Ibid., 57.

21. Quoted in DeVoto, *Journals of Lewis and Clark*, 16.

22. Quoted in Fifer and Soderberg, *Along the Trail*, 61.

23. Ibid.

24. Quoted in Daniel B. Thorp, *Lewis & Clark: An American Journey* (New York: MetroBooks, 1998), 65.

25. Quoted in DeVoto, *Journals of Lewis and Clark*, 123.

26. Quoted in Thorp, *Lewis & Clark*, 70.

CHAPTER 4

27. Quoted in Gillespie, *Wild River*, 5.

28. Ibid.

29. Quoted in Paul O'Neil, *The Rivermen* (New York: TIME-LIFE Books, 1975), 44.

30. Quoted in Gillespie, *Wild River*, 8.

31. Quoted in LeRoy R. Hafen, *Fur Traders, Trappers, and Mountain Men of the Upper Missouri* (Lincoln: University of Nebraska Press, 1965), vii.

32. Ibid., viii.

33. Quoted in R. C. Gildart, *Montana's Missouri River* (Helena: Montana Magazine, Inc., 1979), 20.

34. Ibid., 21.

35. Ibid.

36. Quoted in Barton H. Barbour, *Fort Union and the Upper Missouri Fur Trade* (Norman: University of Oklahoma Press, 2001), 40.

37. Quoted in Gildart, *Montana's Missouri River*, 22.

38. Quoted in Barbour, *Fort Union,* 47.

39. Ibid.

40. Ibid., 60.

41. Quoted in Gildart, *Montana's Missouri River,* 22.

42. Ibid.

43. Quoted in John E. Sunder, *The Fur Trade on the Upper Missouri, 1840–1865* (Norman: University of Oklahoma Press, 1965), 61.

CHAPTER 5
44. Quoted in Gillespie, *Wild River,* 15–16.

45. Ibid.

46. Quoted in O'Neil, *The Rivermen,* 100.

47. Ibid., 100–101.

48. Ibid., 151.

49. Quoted in Gildart, *Montana's Missouri River,* 41.

50. Ibid.

51. Quoted in O'Neil, *The Rivermen,* 104.

52. Quoted in Norbury L. Wayman, *Life on the River: a Pictorial History of the Mississippi, the Missouri, and the Western River System* (New York: Bonanza Books, 1971), 199.

53. Quoted in Gillespie, *Wild River,* 126.

CHAPTER 6
54. Quoted in Gillespie, *Wild River,* 34.

55. Quoted in Schneiders, *Unruly River,* 55.

56. Ibid., 60.

57. Ibid., 62.

58. Ibid., 69.

59. Ibid., 77.

60. Ibid., 89.

61. Ibid., 98.

62. Ibid., 114.

63. Ibid., 128.

64. Ibid.

65. Ibid., 138.

66. Ibid., 139.

67. To be supplied by author.

CHAPTER 7
68. Quoted in Schneiders, *Unruly River,* 162.

69. Ibid., 167.

70. Quoted in "Flood Control More Than a Dream," *Sioux City Journal,* August 24, 1943, 7.

71. Ibid.

72. Quoted in Schneiders, *Unruly River,* 171.

73. Ibid., 180.

74. Ibid., 189.

75. Ibid., 195.

76. Ibid., 227.

77. Ibid.

78. Ibid., 235.

79. Ibid., 247.

80. Ibid., 251.

81. Quoted in Vestal, *The Missouri,* 332.

Ambrose, Stephen. *Undaunted Courage: Meriwether Lewis, Thomas Jefferson, and the Opening of the American West.* New York: Simon & Schuster, 1996.

"America Looks West: Lewis and Clark on the Missouri," *Nebraskaland Magazine,* 80, no. 7 (August–September, 2002): .

Barbour, Barton H. *Fort Union and the Upper Missouri Fur Trade.* Norman: University of Oklahoma Press, 2001.

Bloch, E. Maurice. *The Paintings of George Caleb Bingham: A Catalogue Raisonné.* Columbia: University of Missouri Press, 1986.

Botkin, Daniel B. *Passage of Discovery: The American Rivers Guide to the Missouri River of Lewis and Clark.* New York: Perigee Books, 1999.

"The Cellars of Time: Paleontology and Archaeology in Nebraska," *Nebraska History,* 75, no. 1 (Spring 1994): .

DeVoto, Bernard, ed. *The Journals of Lewis and Clark.* Boston: Houghton Mifflin, 1981, (reprint).

Fifer, Barbara, and Vicky Soderberg. *Along the Trail With Lewis and Clark.* Helena: Montana Magazine, Inc., 2001.

"Flood Control More Than a Dream," *Sioux City Journal,* August 24, 1943, 7.

Gildart, R. C. *Montana's Missouri River.* Helena: Montana Magazine, Inc., 1979.

Gillespie, Michael. *Wild River, Wooden Boats: True Stories of Steamboating and the Missouri River.* Stoddard, WI: Heritage Press, 2000.

Hafen, LeRoy R. *Fur Traders, Trappers, and Mountain Men of the Upper Missouri.* Lincoln: University of Nebraska Press, 1965.

Josephy, Alvin M., Jr. *The Indian Heritage of America.* Boston: Houghton Mifflin, 1991.

Larsen, Lawrence H., and Barbara J. Cottrell. *The Gate City: A History of Omaha.* Lincoln: University of Nebraska Press, 1997.

Nagel, Paul C. *Missouri, A History.* Lawrence: University Press of Kansas, 1977.

O'Neil, Paul. *The Rivermen.* New York: TIME-LIFE Books, 1975.

Schmidt, Jeremy, and Thomas Schmidt. *The Saga of Lewis & Clark into the Uncharted West.* New York: DK Publishing, 1999.

Schmidt, Thomas. *National Geographic Guide to the Lewis & Clark Trail.* Washington, DC: National Geographic Society, 2002.

Schneiders, Robert Kelley. *Unruly River: Two Centuries of Change Along the Missouri.* Lawrence: University Press of Kansas, 1999.

Sunder, John E. *The Fur Trade on the Upper Missouri, 1840–1865.* Norman: University of Oklahoma Press, 1965.

Thorne, Tanis C. *The Many Hands of My Relations: French and Indians on the Lower Missouri.* Columbia: University of Missouri Press, 1996.

Thorp, Daniel B. *Lewis & Clark: An American Journey.* New York: MetroBooks, 1998.

Vestal, Stanley. *The Missouri.* Lincoln: University of Nebraska Press, 1945.

Wayman, Norbury L. *Life on the River. A Pictorial History of the Mississippi, The Missouri, and the Western River System.* New York: Bonanza Books, 1971.

Wheeler, Keith. *The Chroniclers.* New York: TIME-LIFE Books, 1976.

Wood, W. Raymond. *Prologue to Lewis and Clark: The Mackay and Evans Expedition.* Norman: University of Oklahoma Press, 2003.

page:

5: © Historical Picture Archive/CORBIS
11: National Park Service
16: © Hulton|Archive by Getty Images, Inc.
20: © Geoffrey Clements/CORBIS
26: Library of Congress
33: © Bettmann/CORBIS
38: © Historical Picture Archive/CORBIS
46: National Park Service
50: © CORBIS

54: © David Muench/CORBIS
65: © Historical Picture Archive/CORBIS
67: NOAA Photo Library, archival photo-
    graph by Mr. Sean Linehan
72: Library of Congress
76: © Charles E. Rotkin/CORBIS
81: © Najlah Feanny/CORBIS SABA
84: © Scott T. Smith/CORBIS

Cover: © David Muench/CORBIS
Frontis: Library of Congress, digital ID g4125 ct000683

TIM MCNEESE is an Associate Professor of History at York College in Nebraska. Professor McNeese earned an Associate of Arts degree from York College, a Bachelor of Arts degree in history and political science from Harding University, and a Master of Arts degree in history from Southwest Missouri State University. He is currently in his 27th year of teaching.

Professor McNeese's writing career has earned him a citation in the "Something About the Author" reference work. He is the author of more than fifty books and educational materials on everything from Egyptian pyramids to American Indians. He is married to Beverly McNeese, who teaches English at York College.